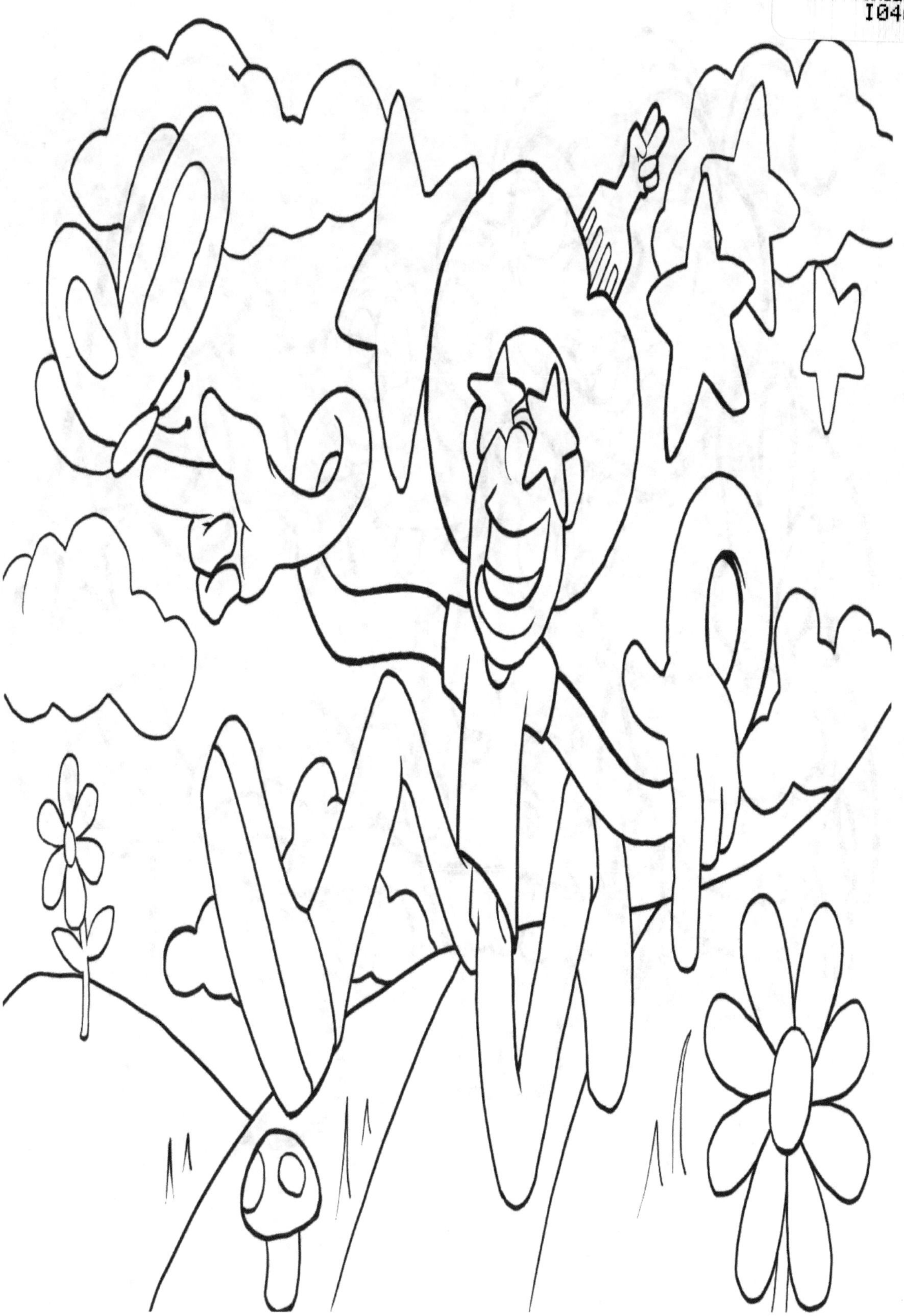

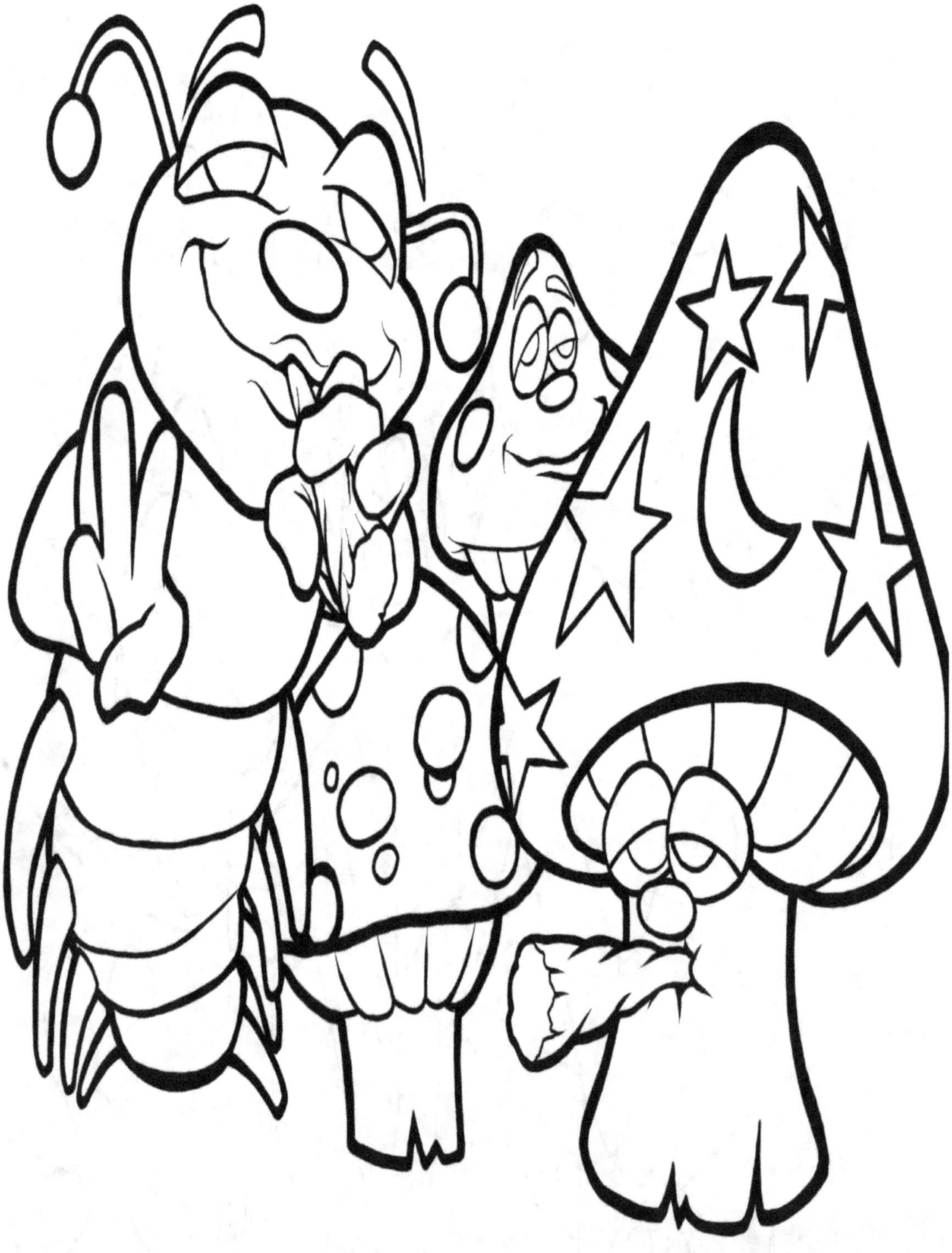

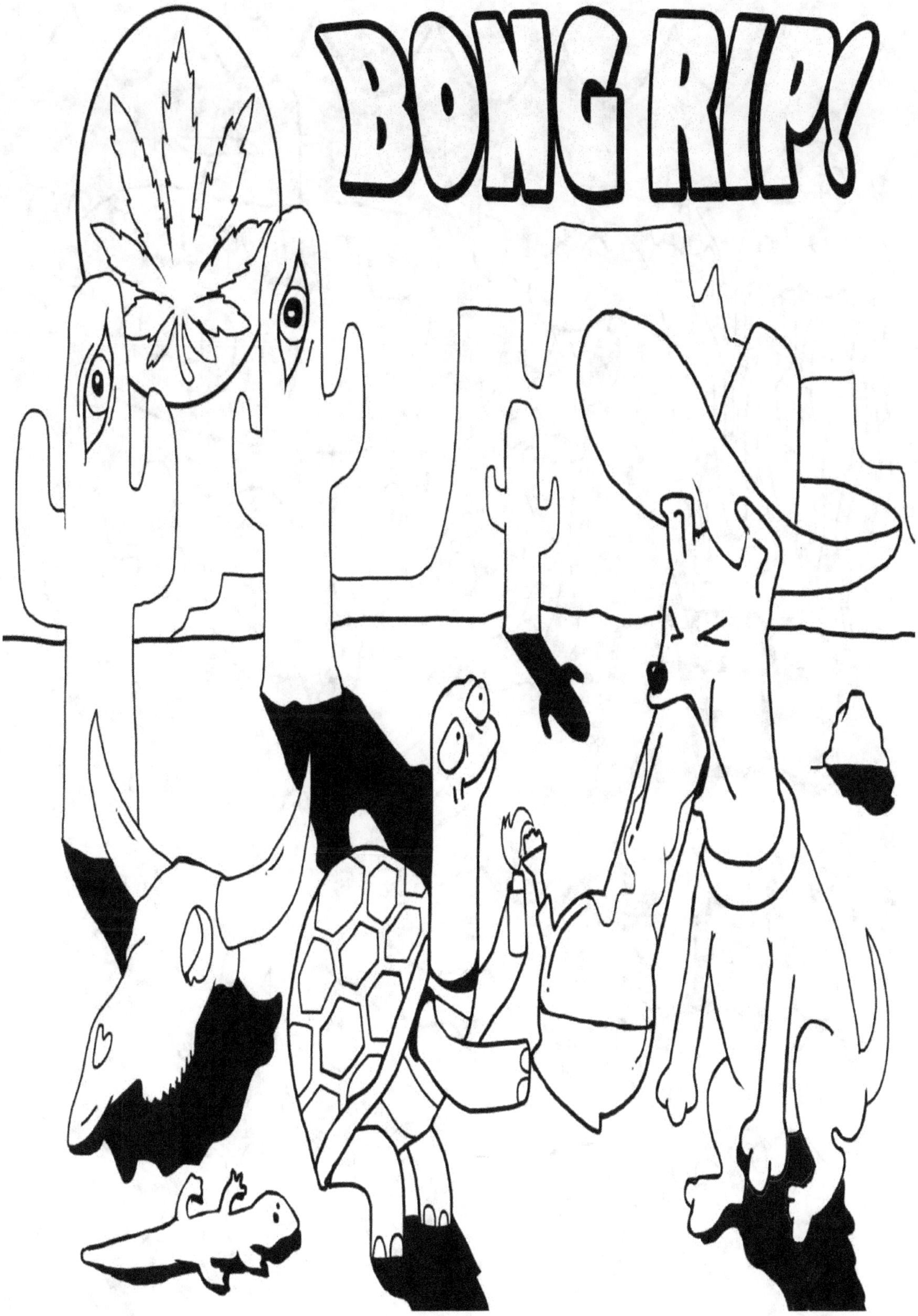
BONG RIP!

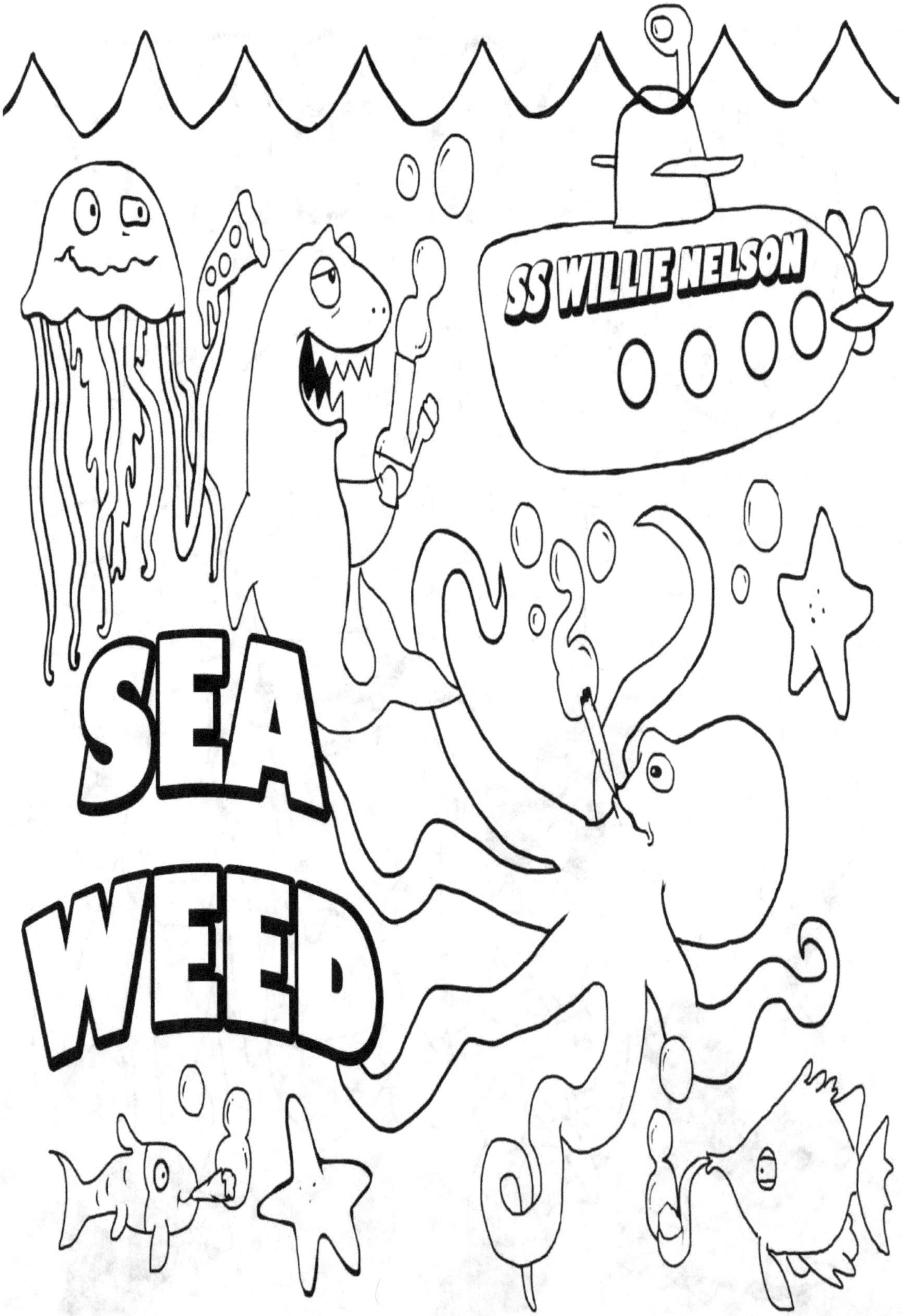
SS WILLIE NELSON
SEA
WEED

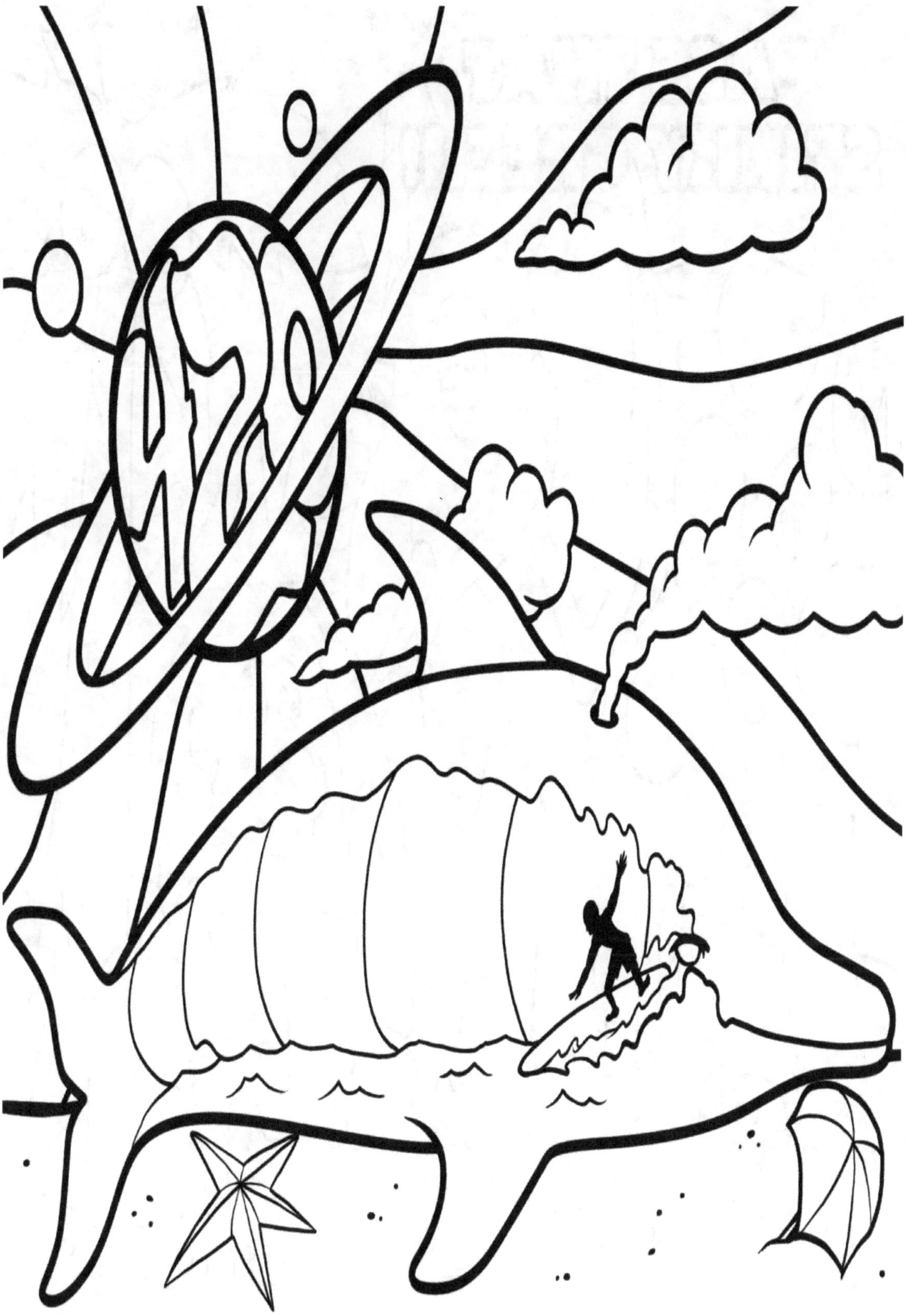
H2O

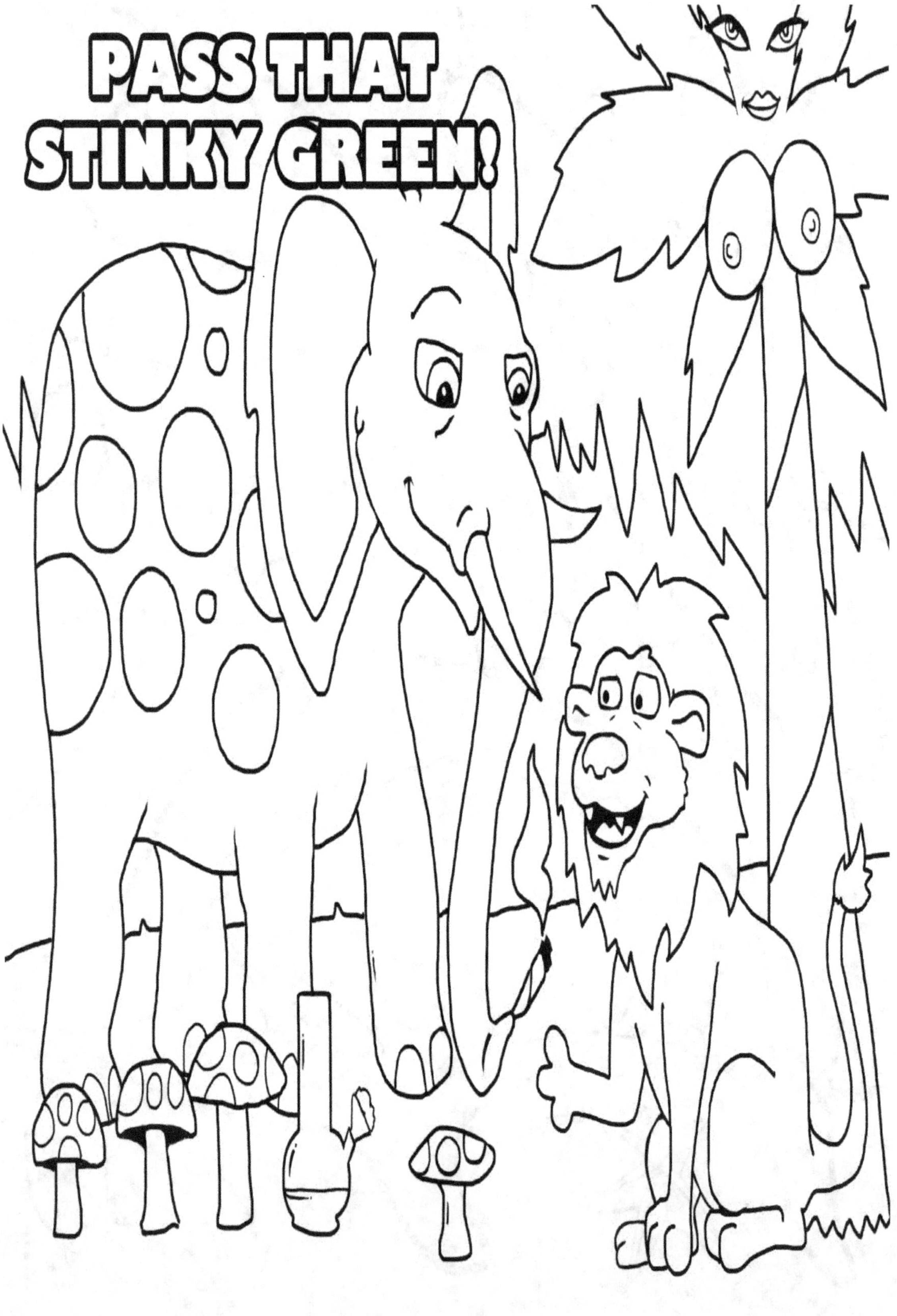
PASS THAT
STINKY GREEN!

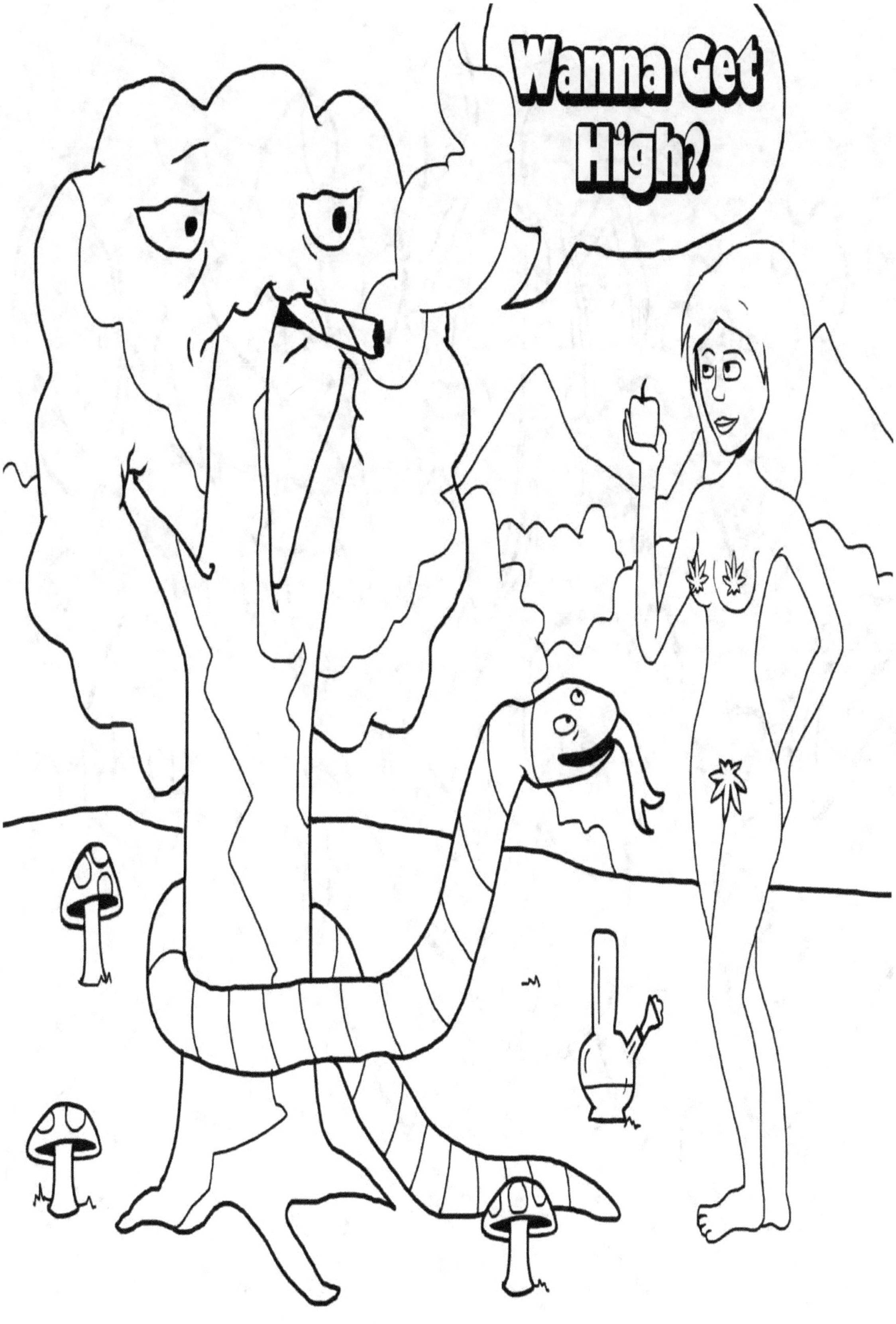
Wanna Get High?

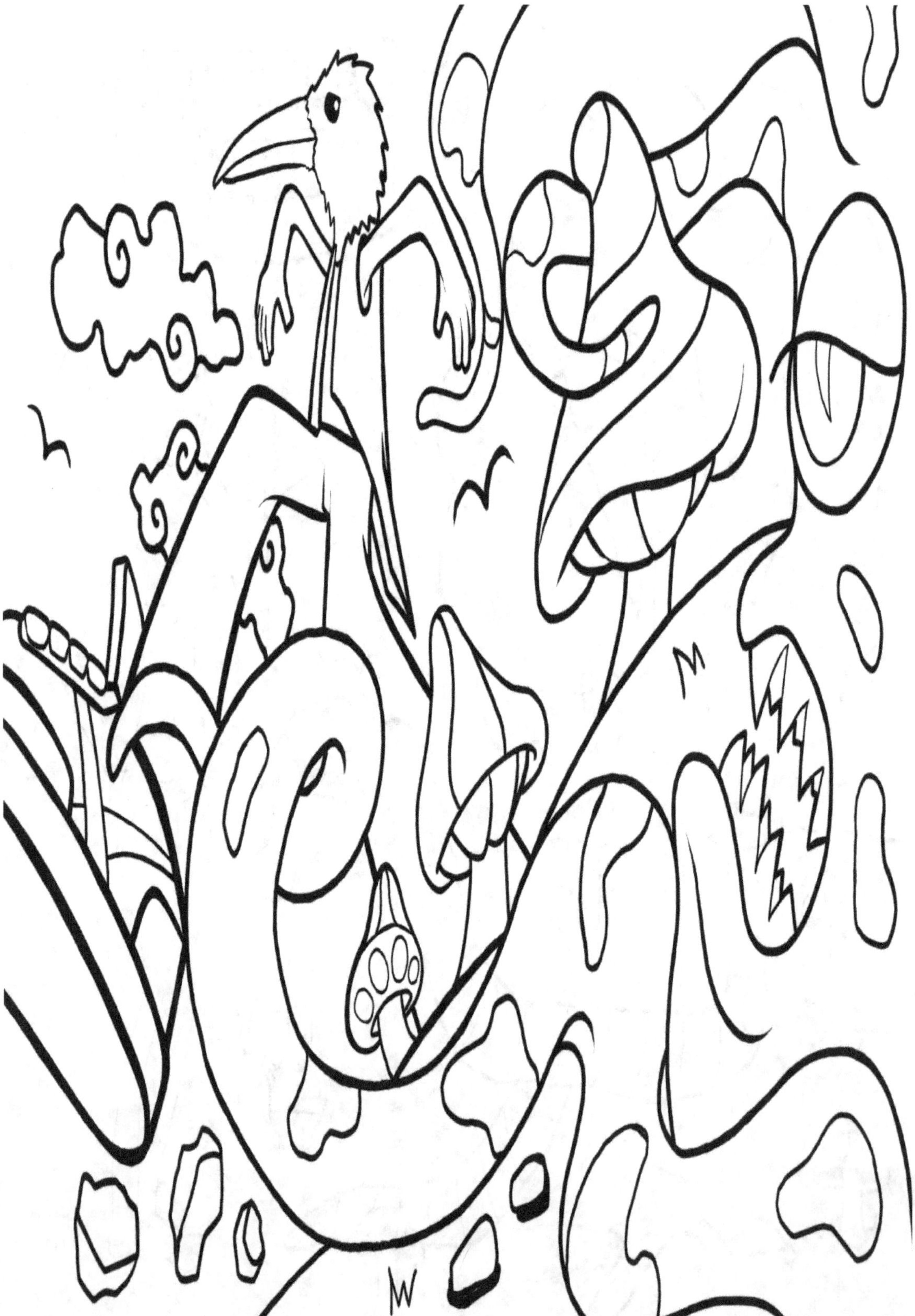

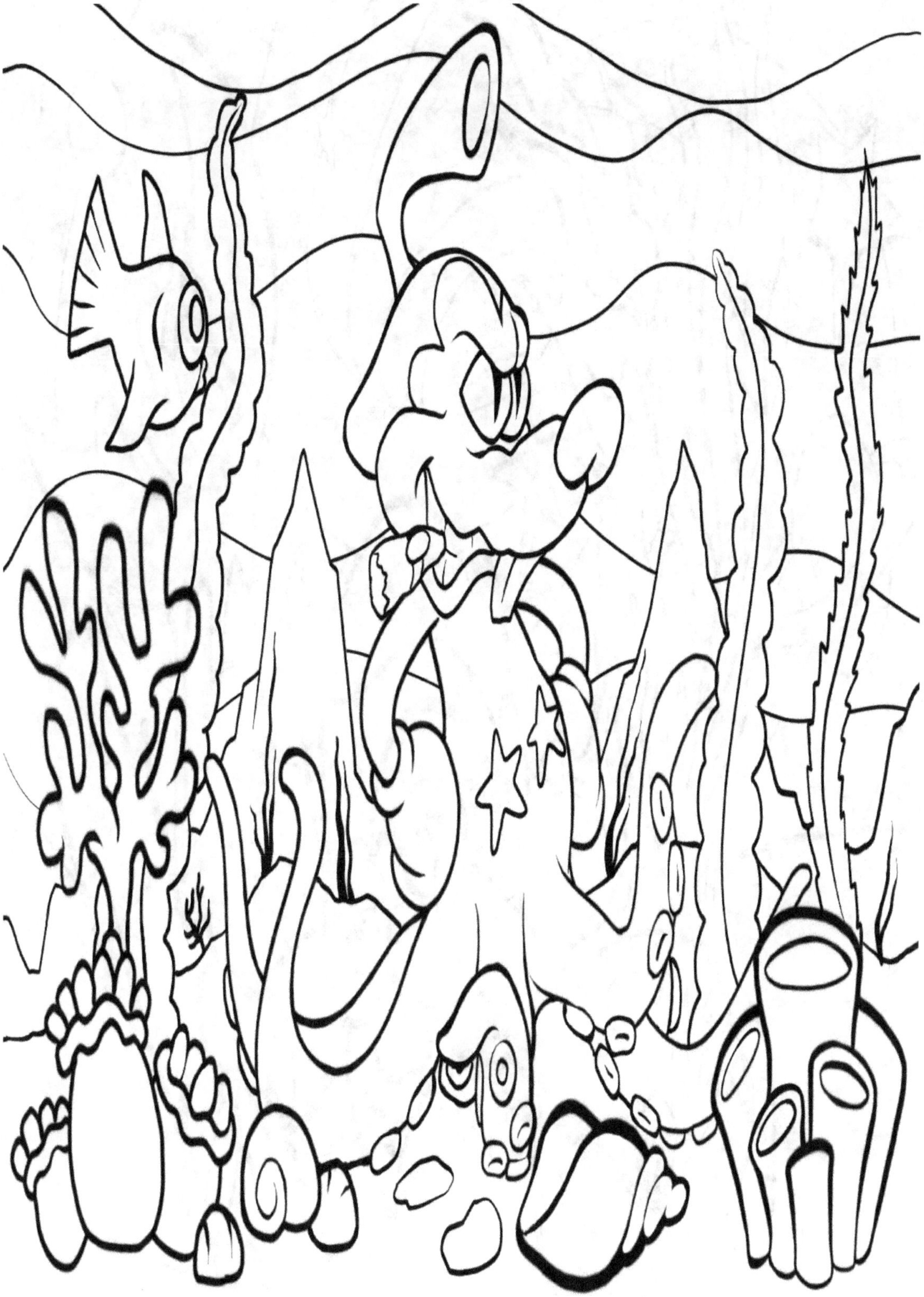

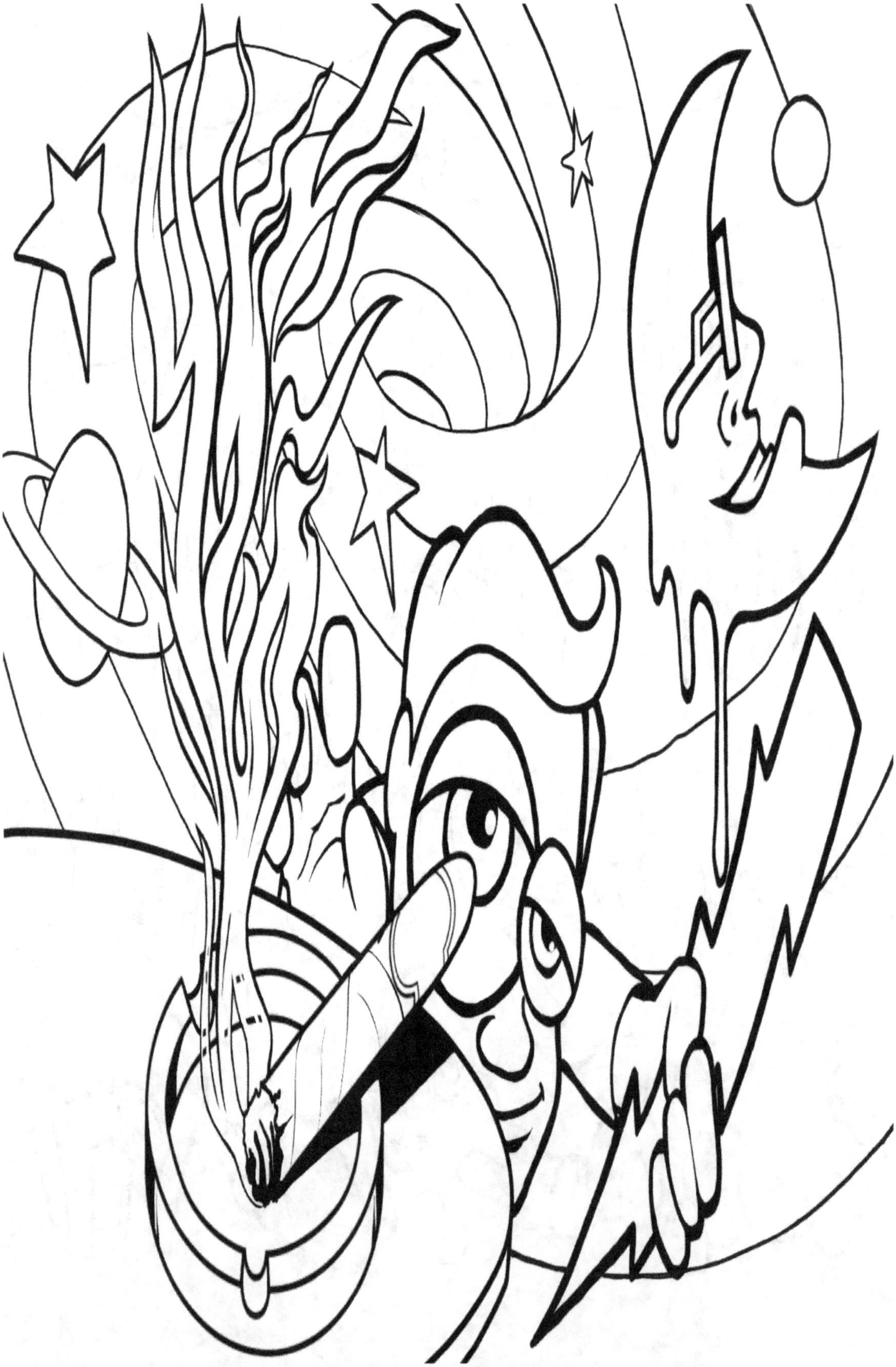

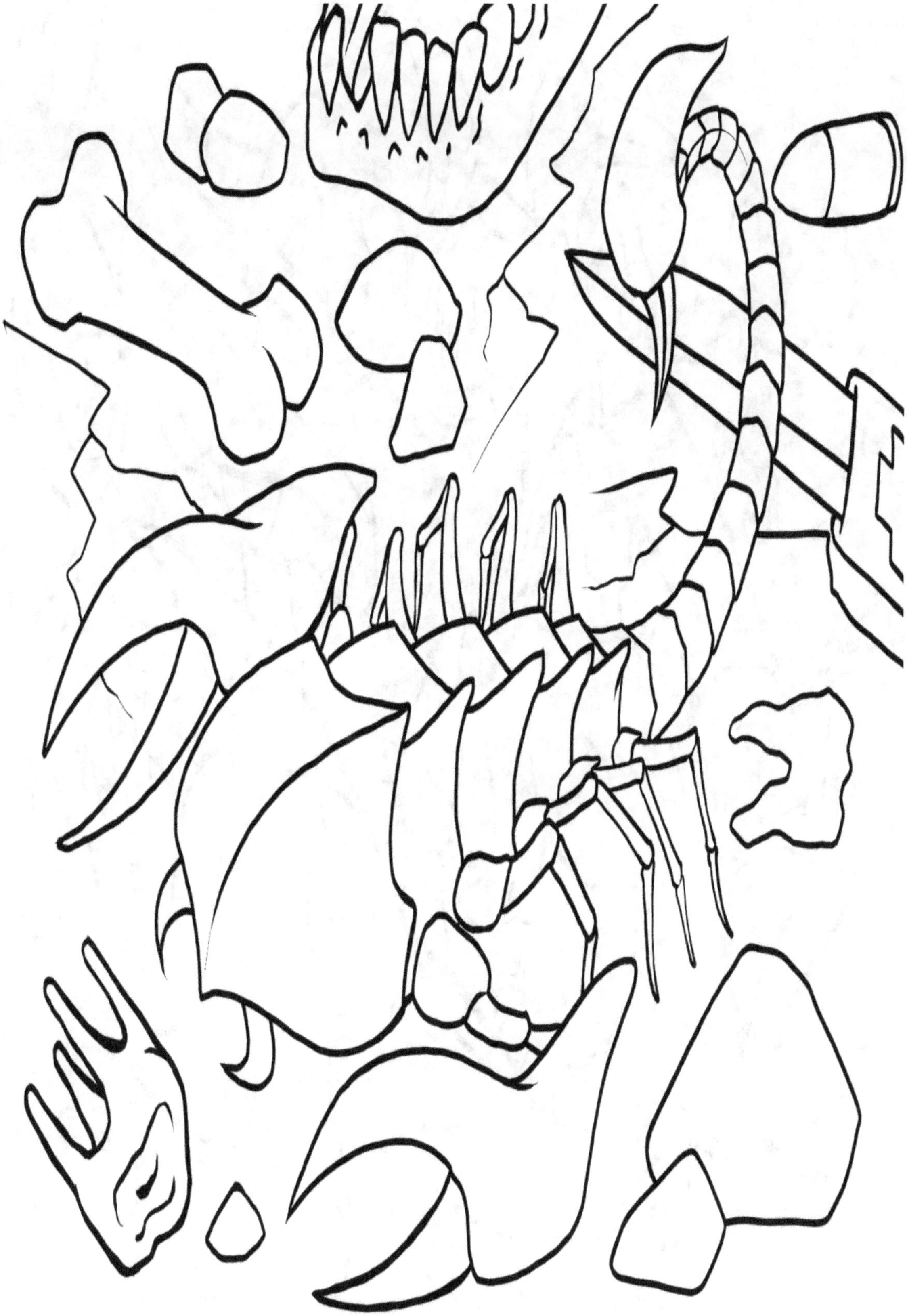

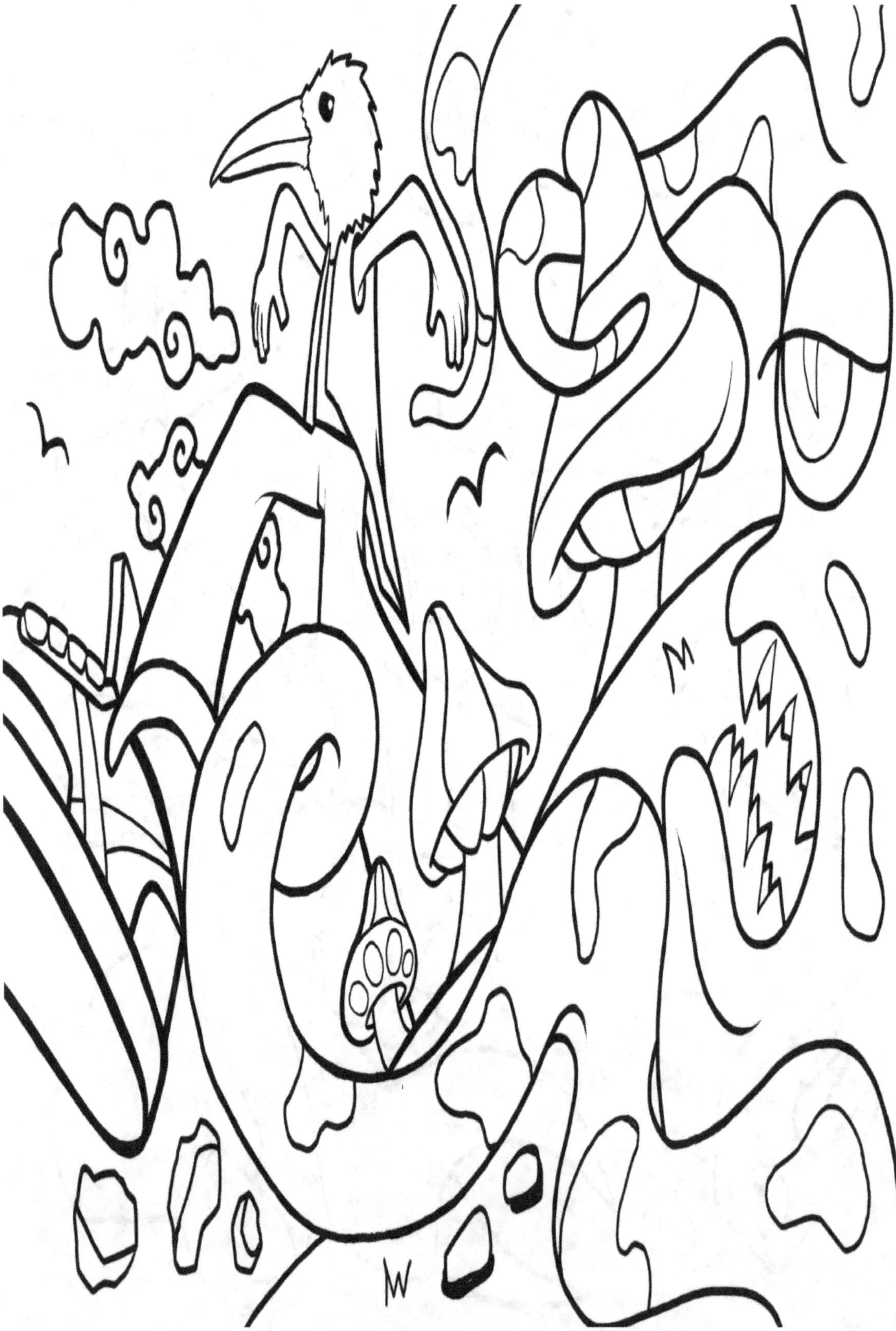

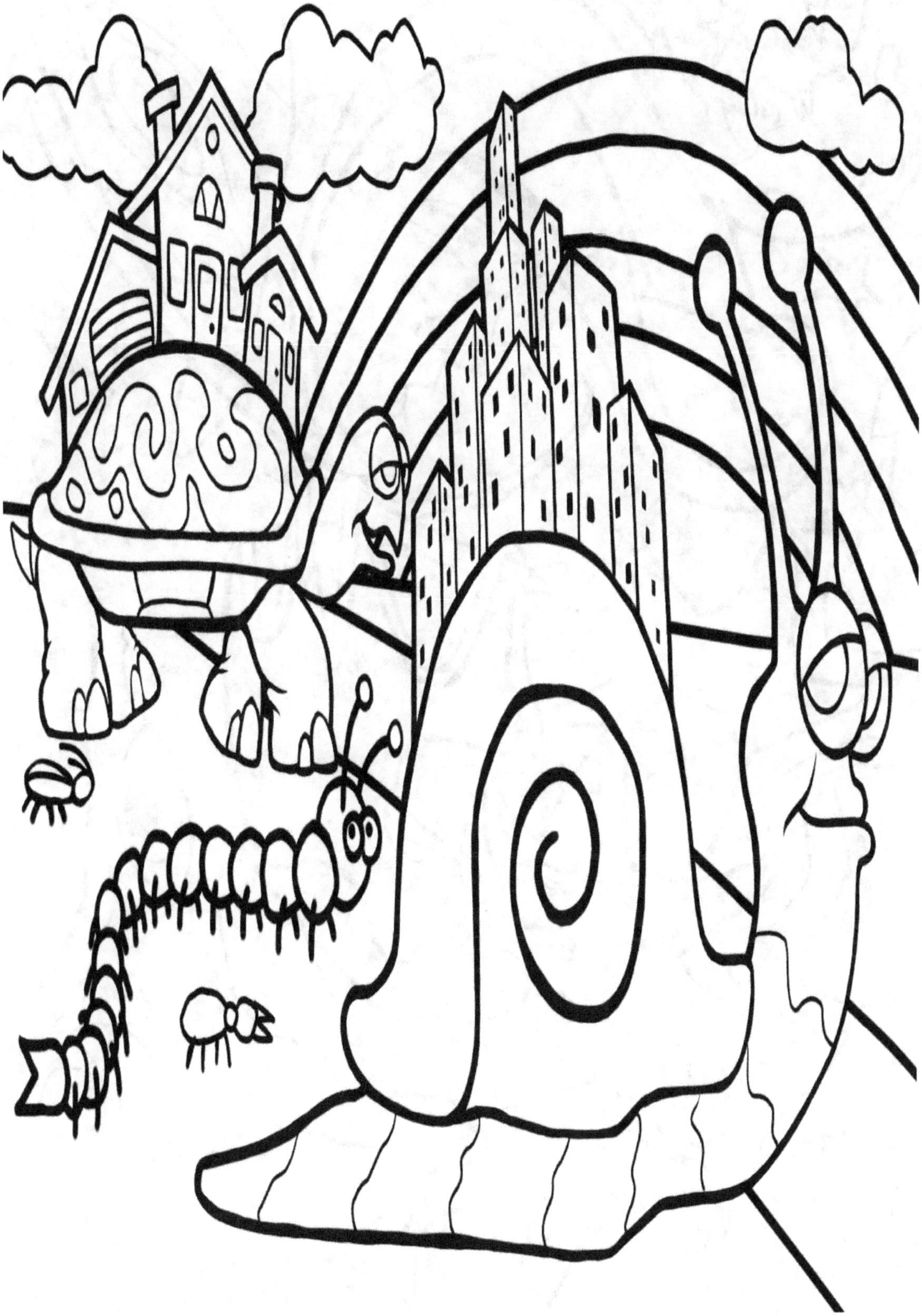

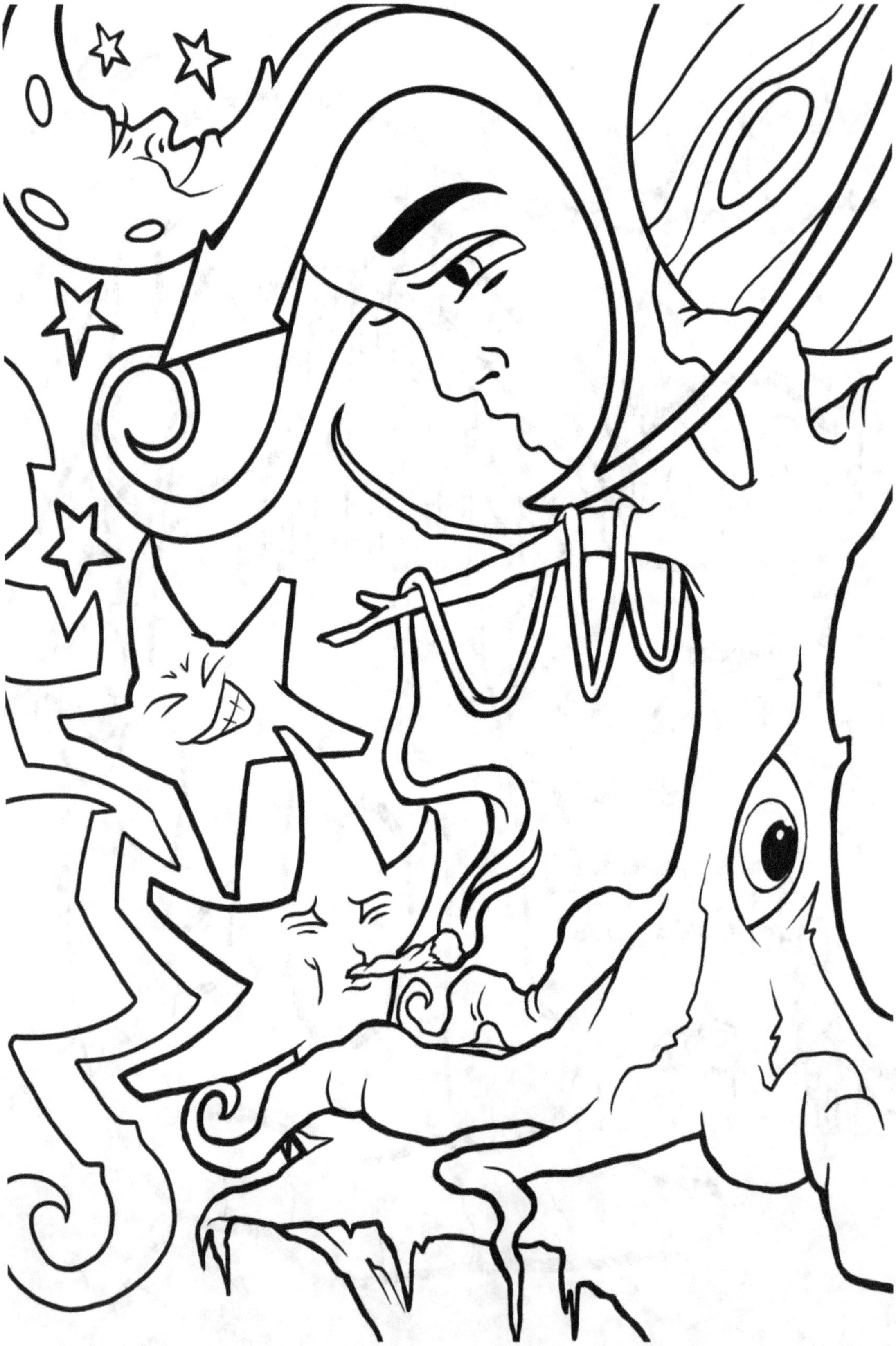

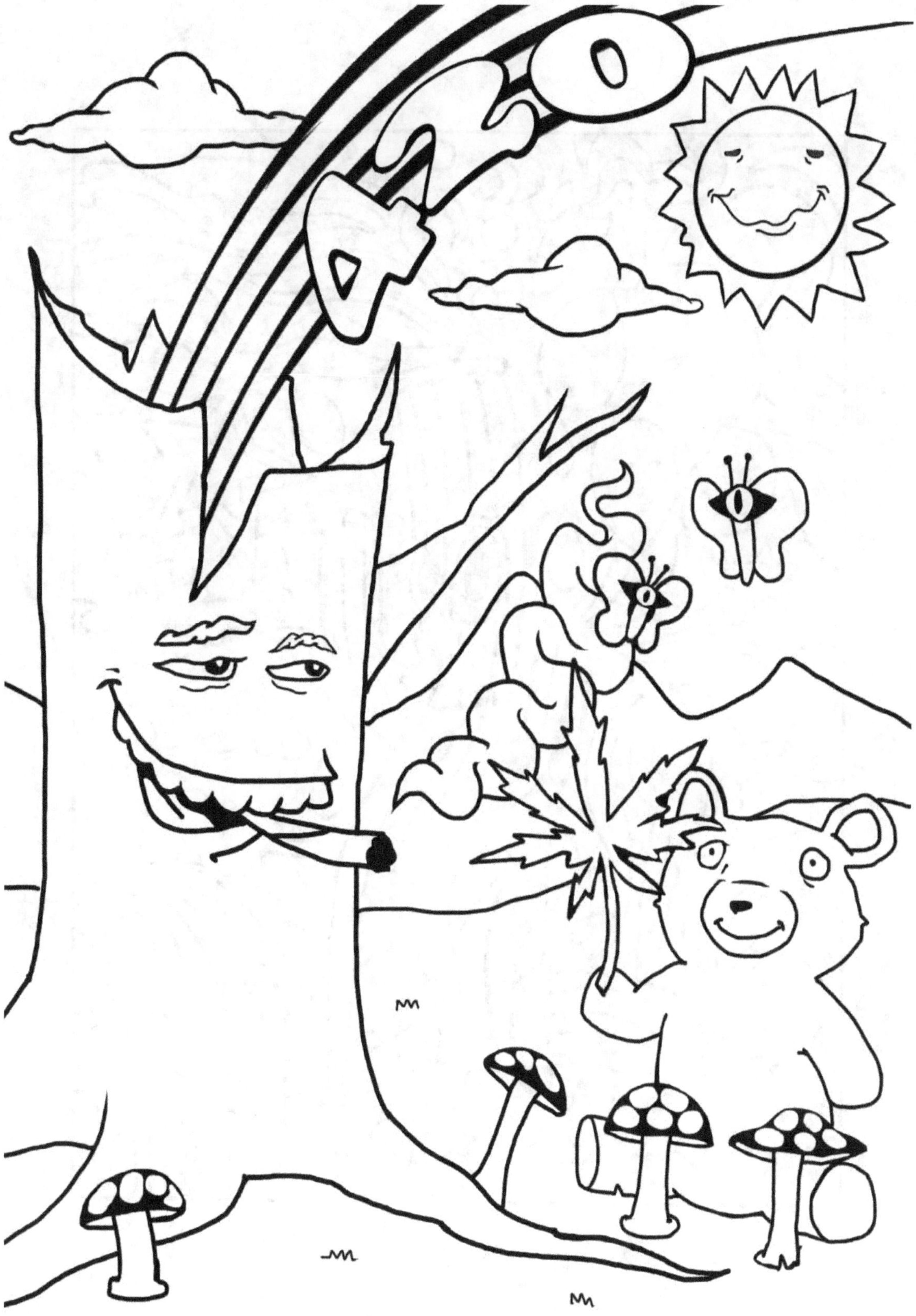

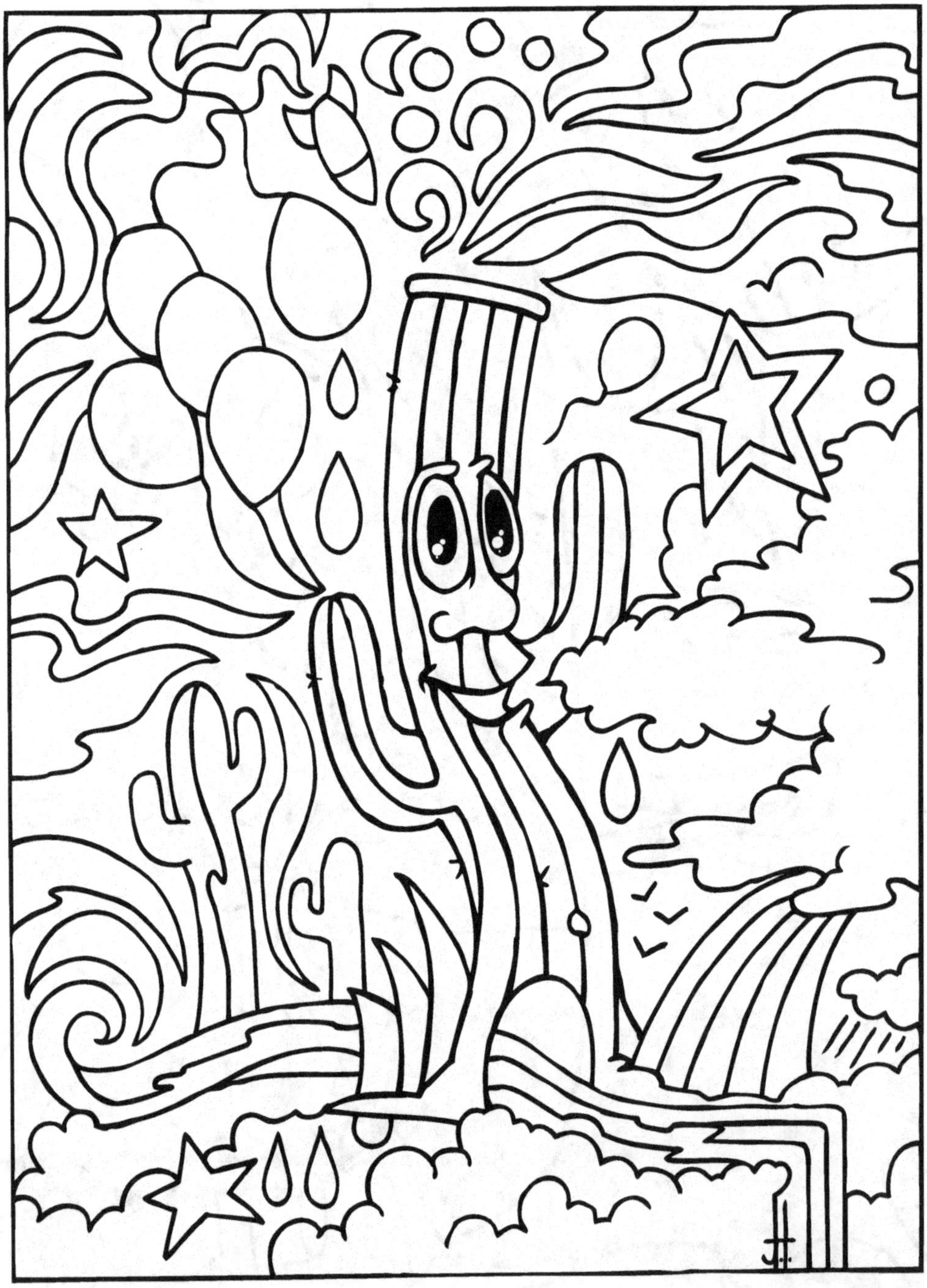

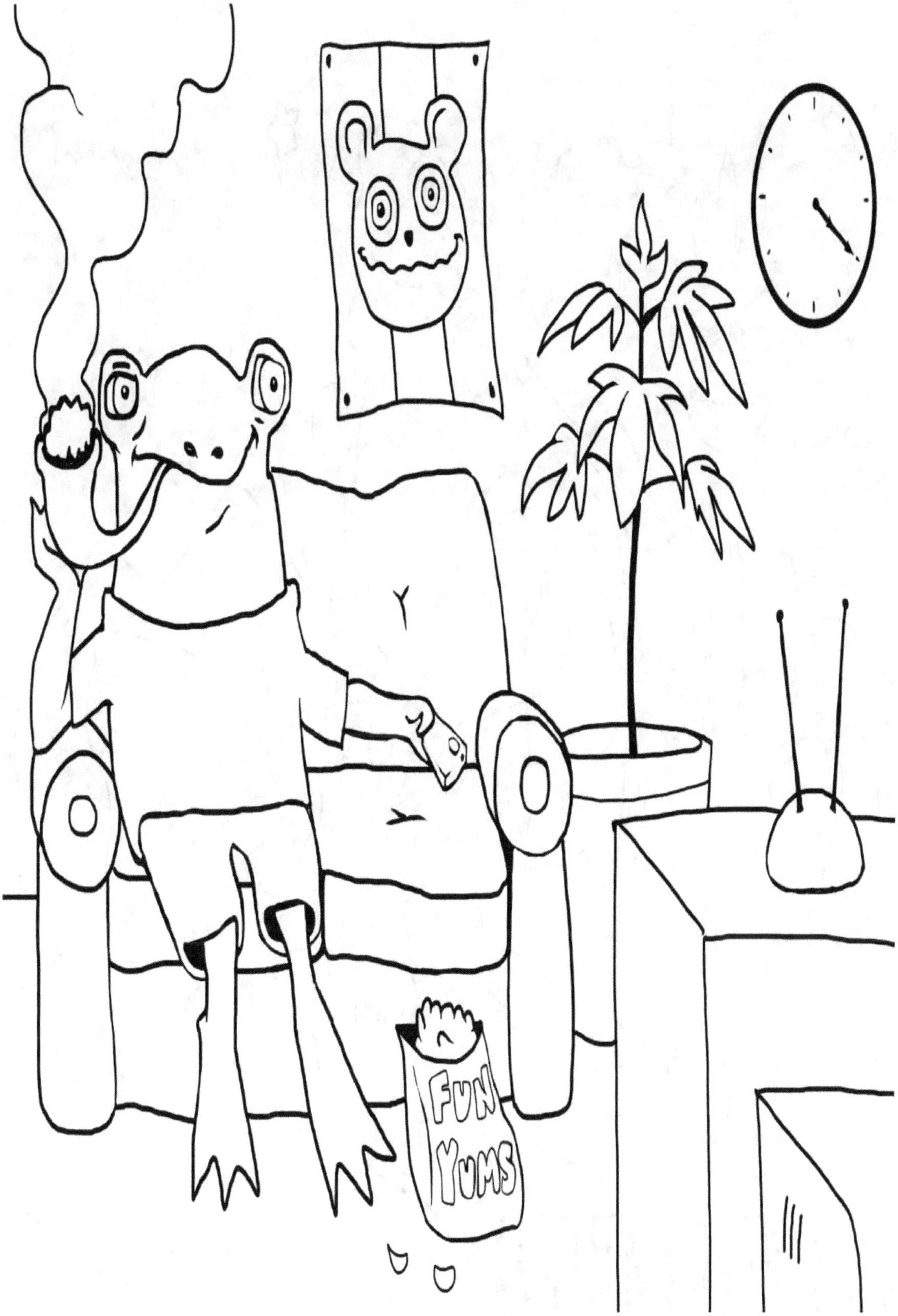
FUN
YUMS

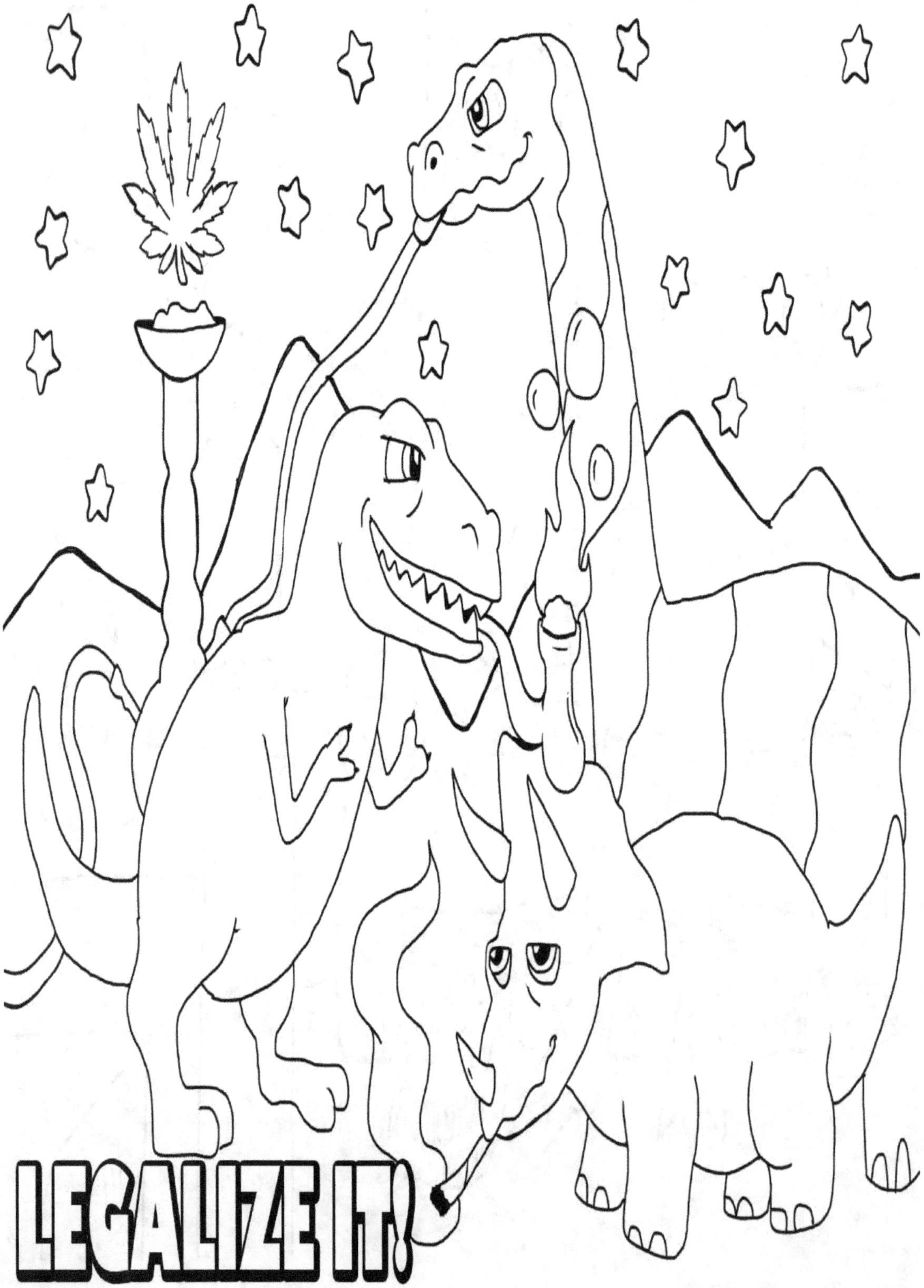
LEGALIZE IT!

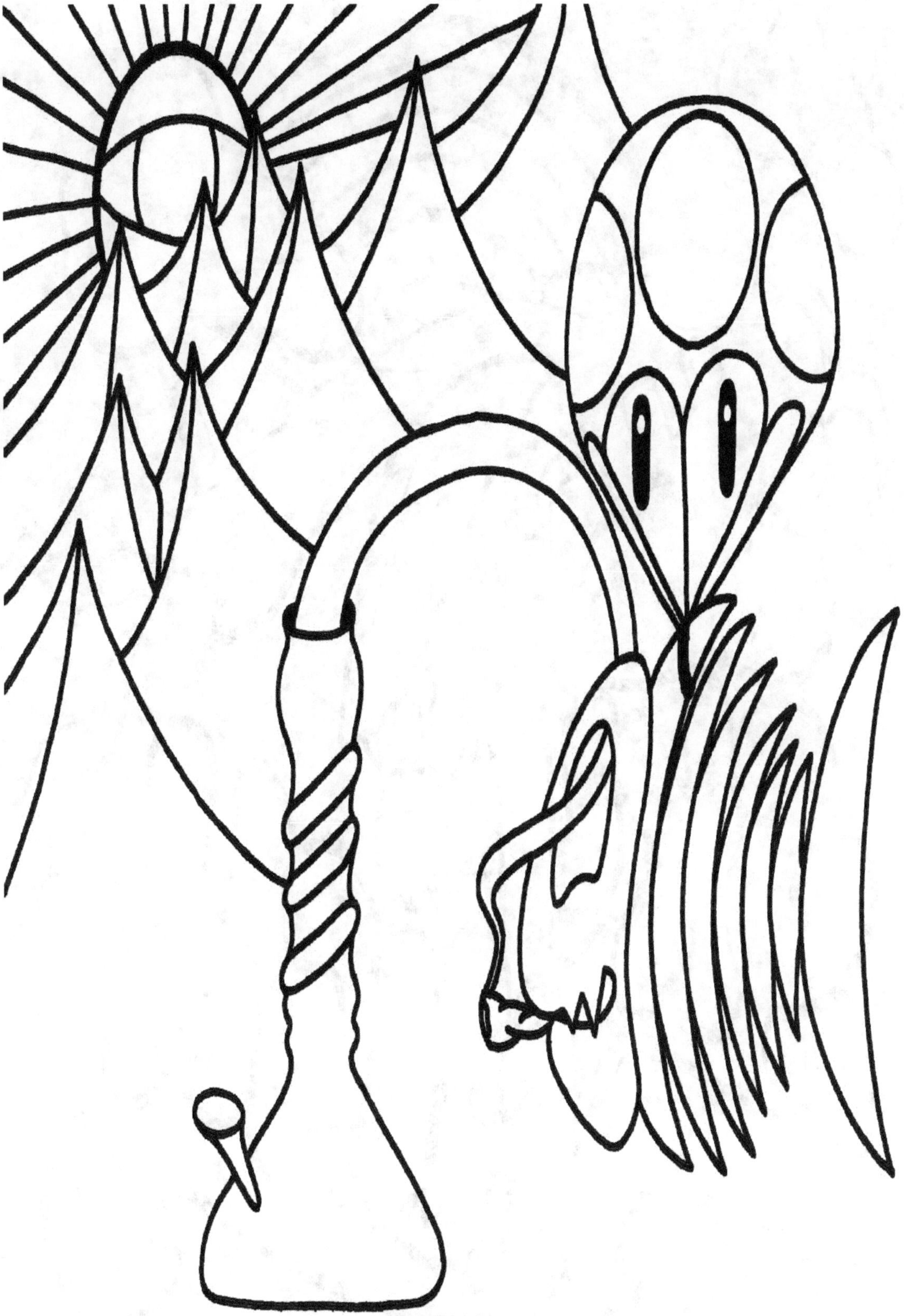

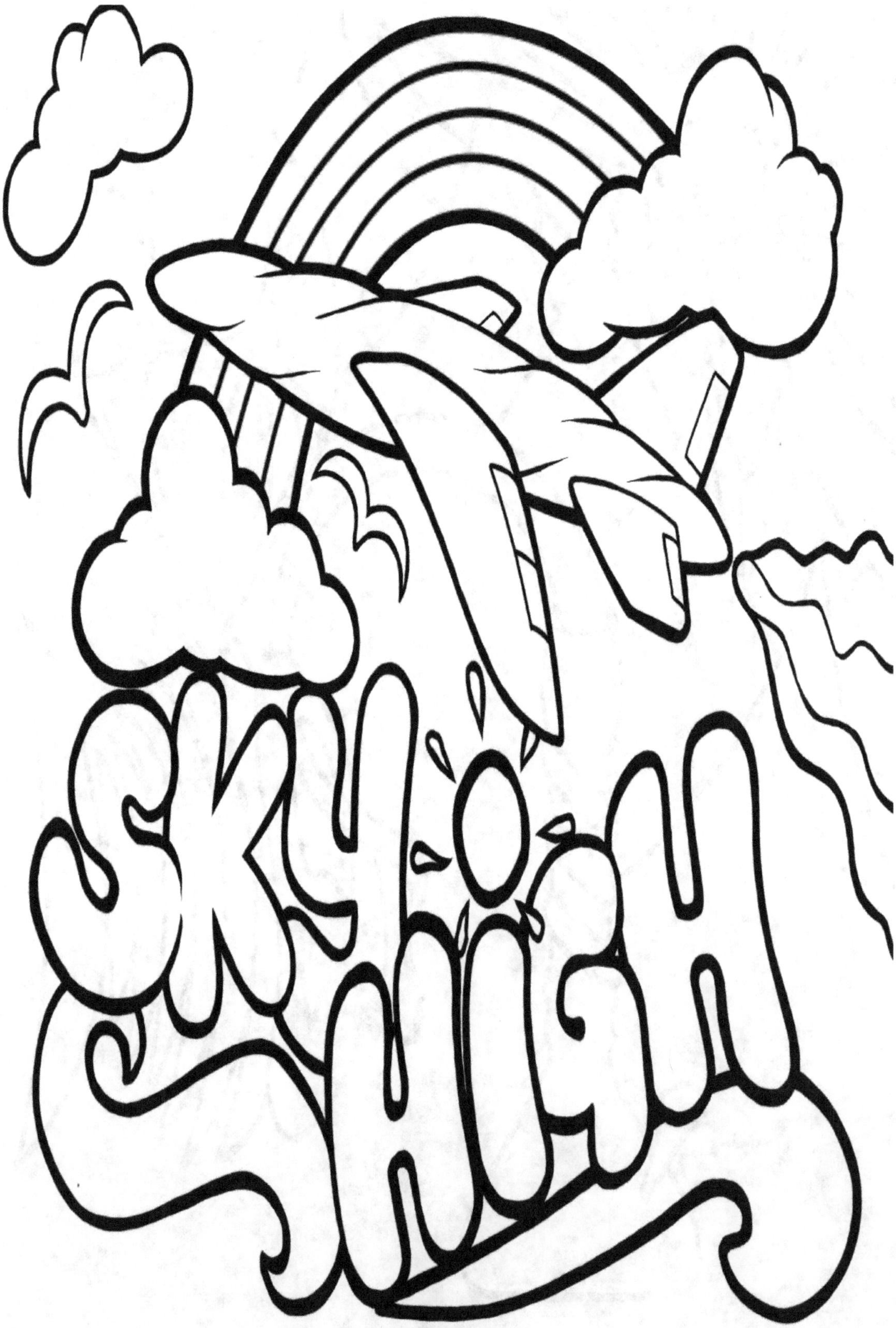
SKY-HIGH

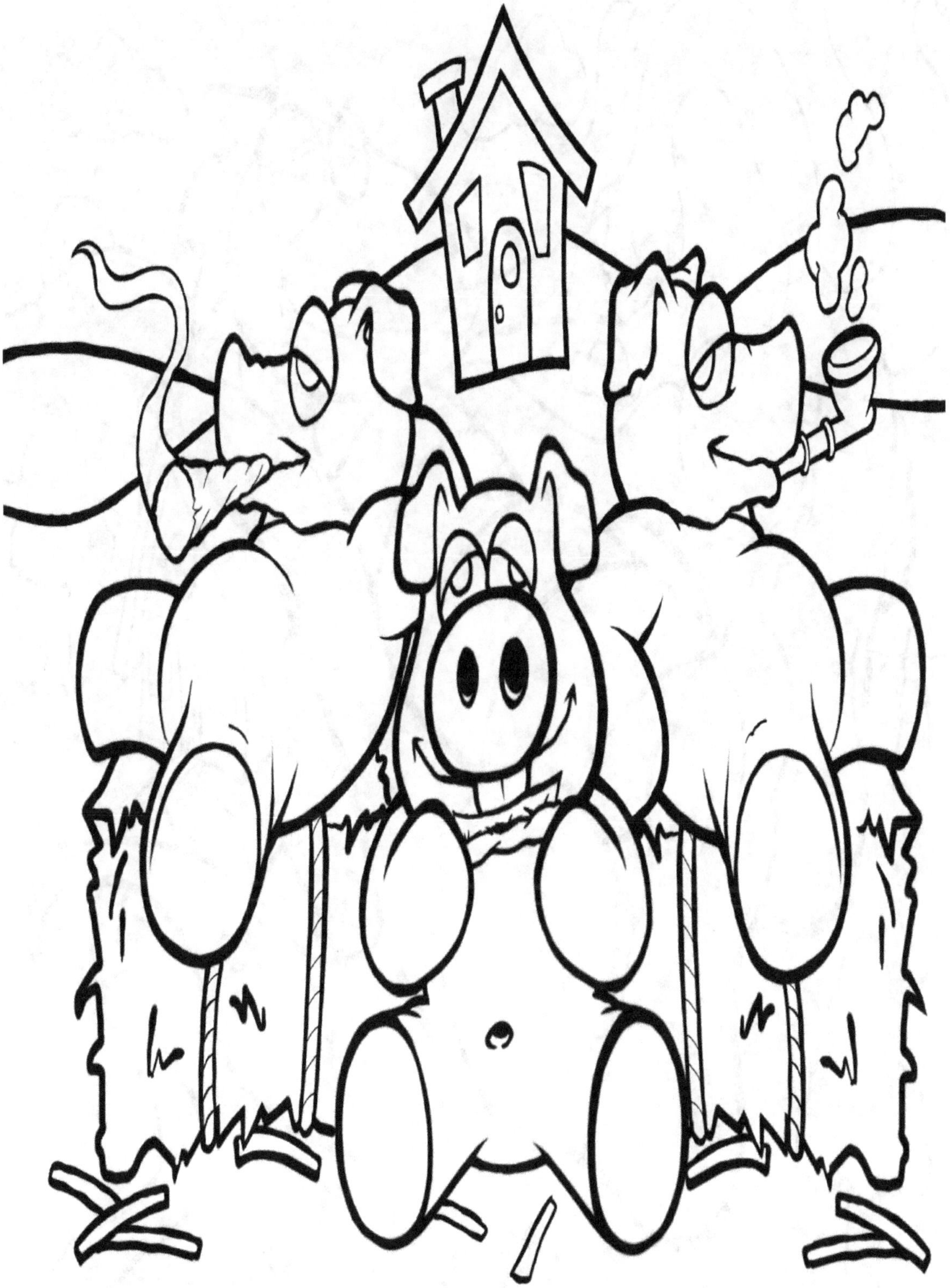

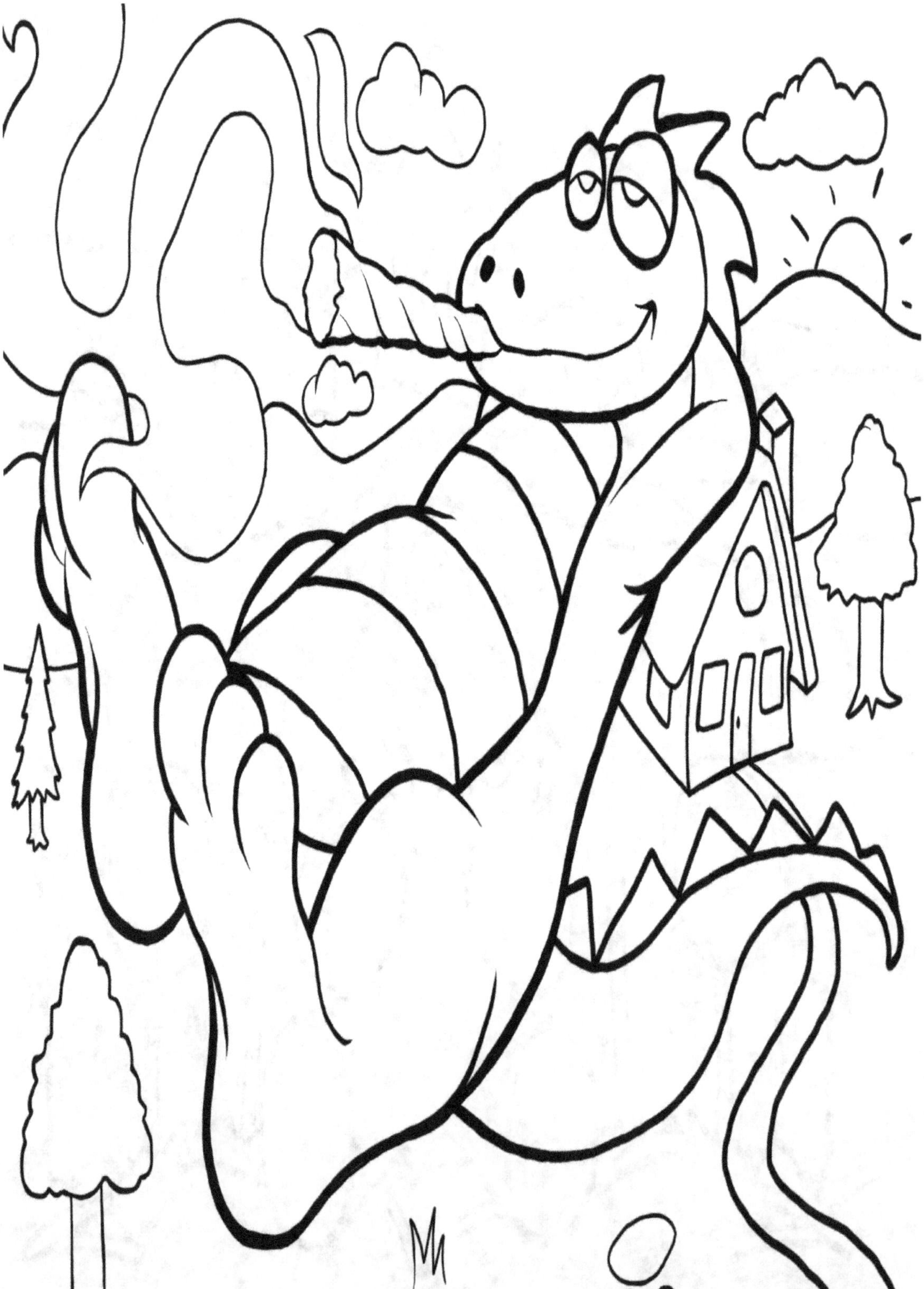

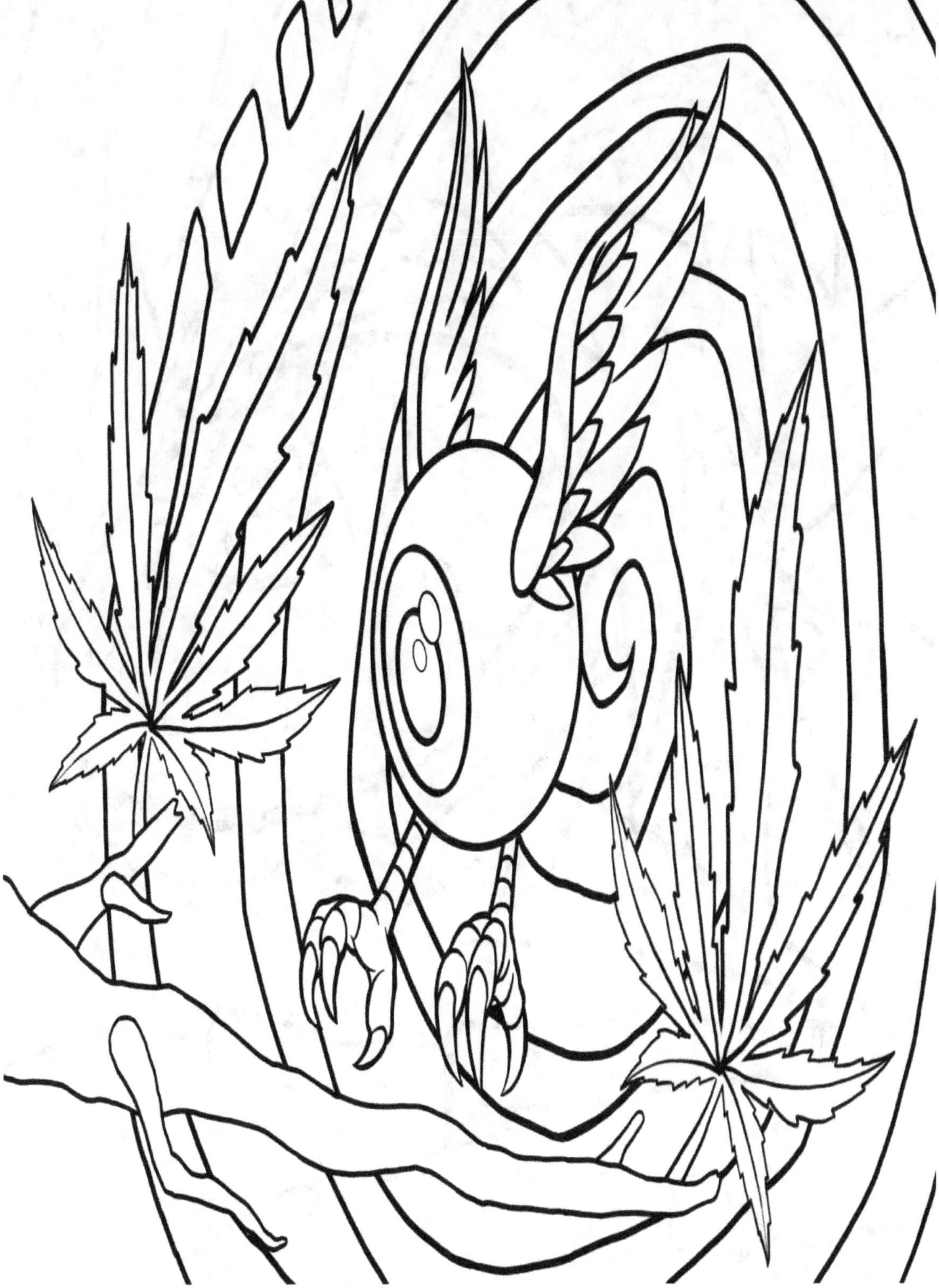

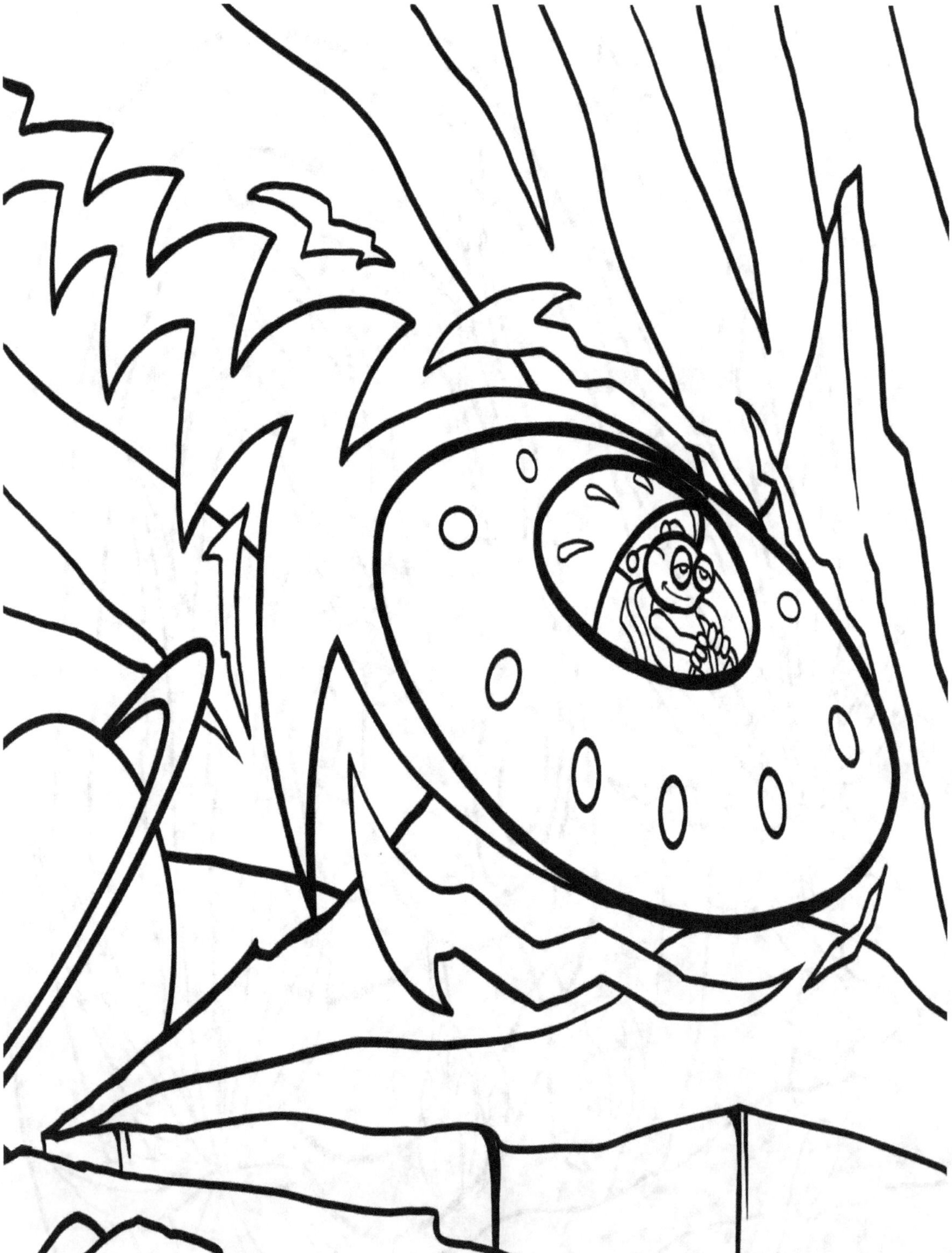

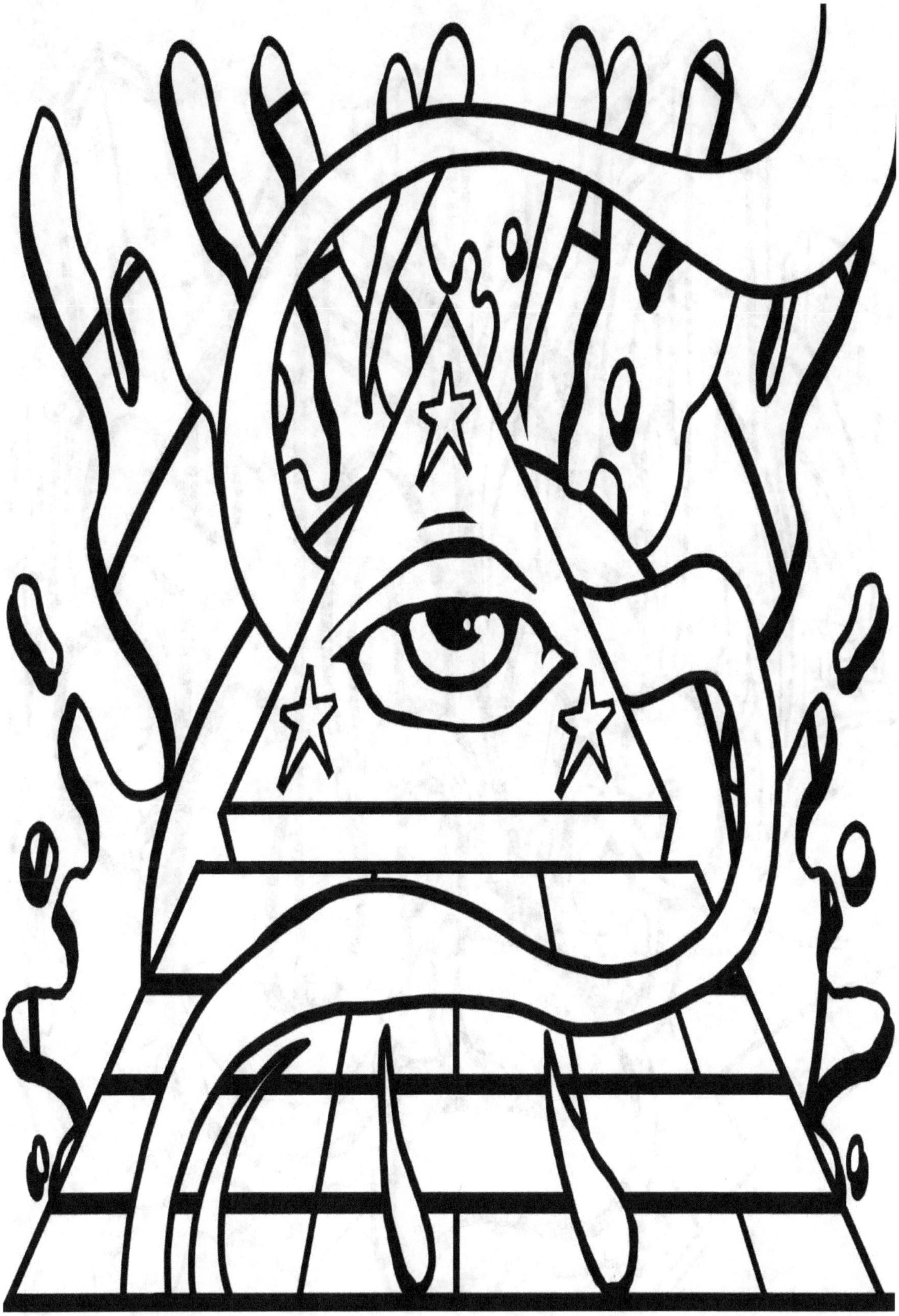

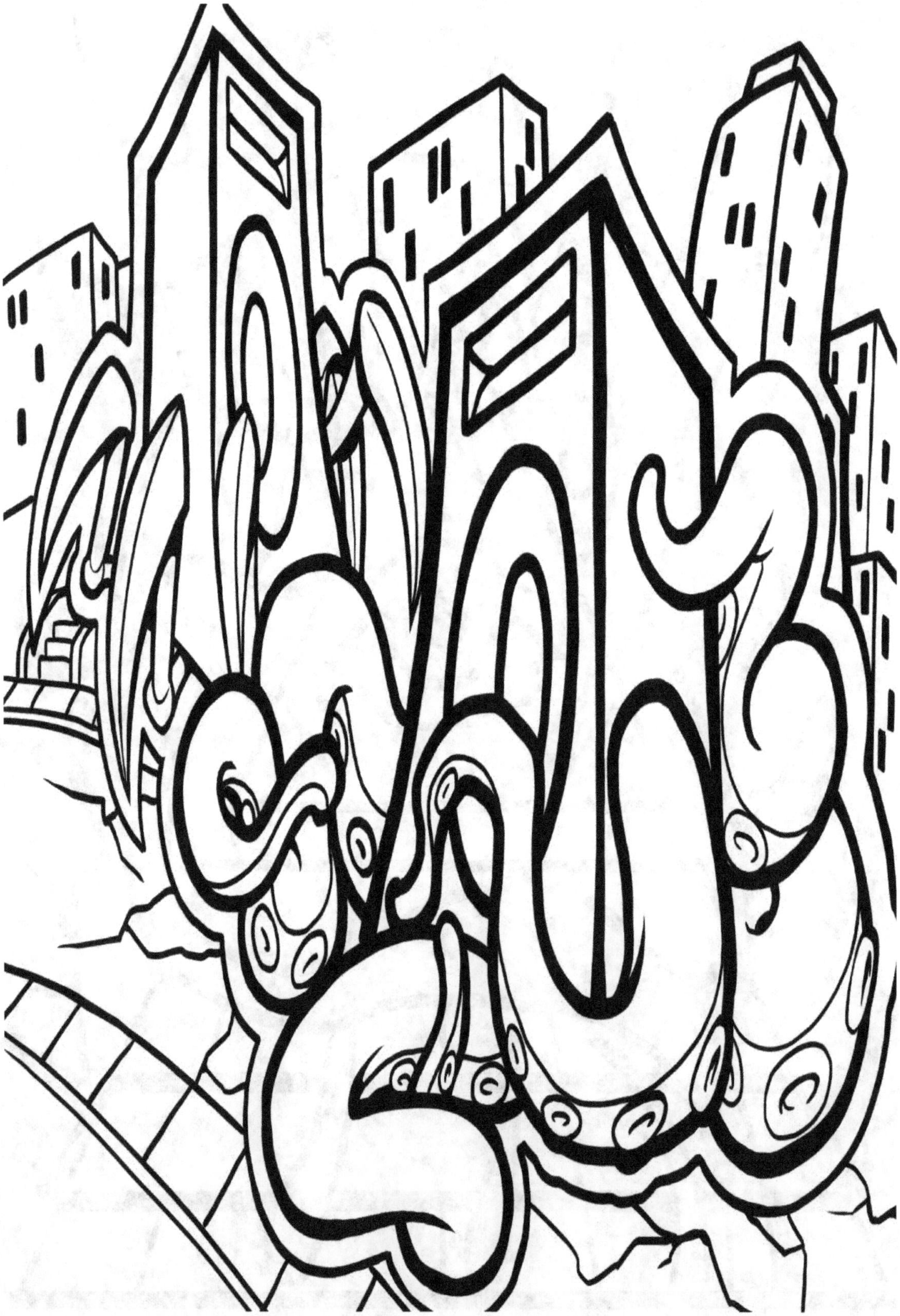

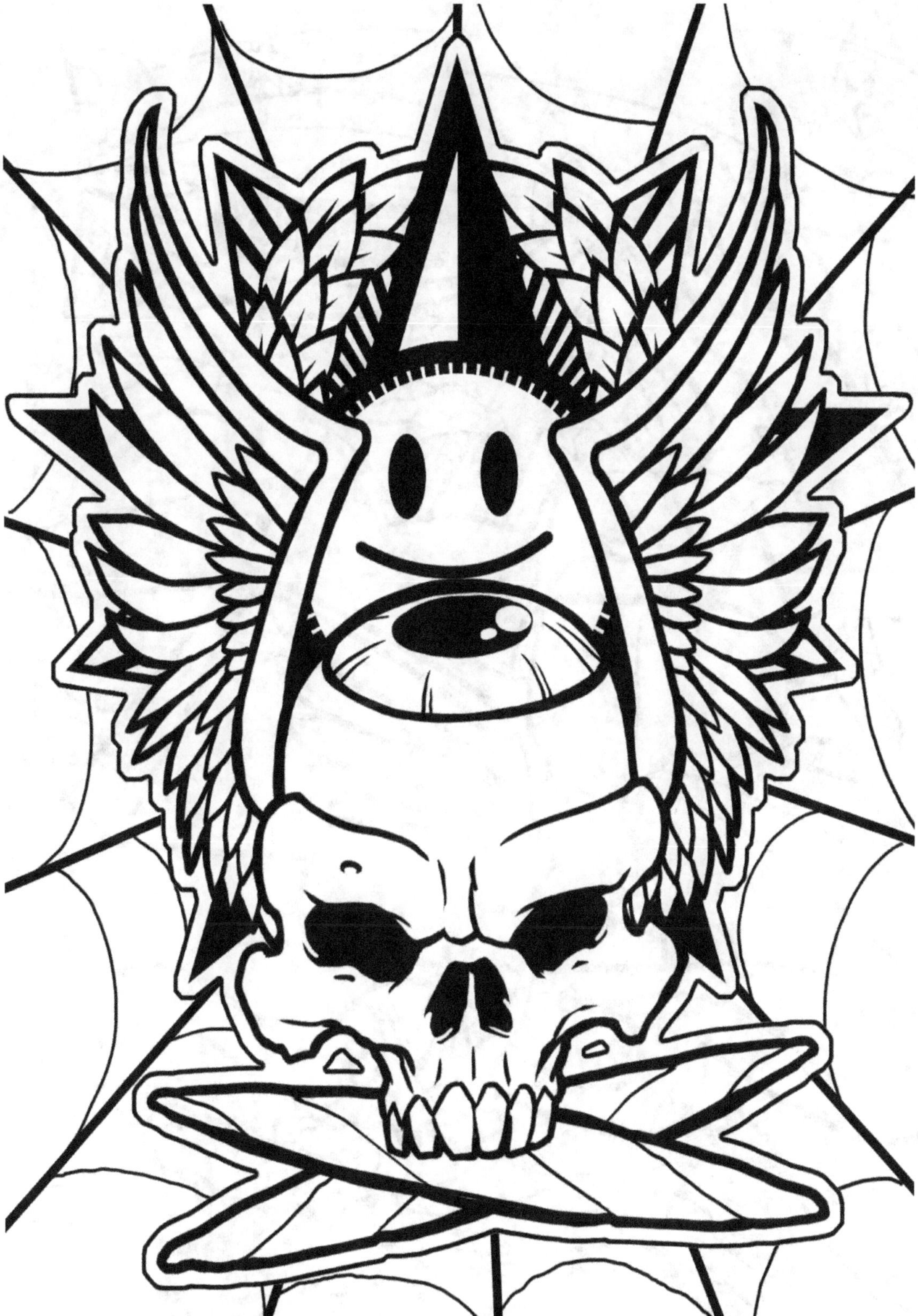

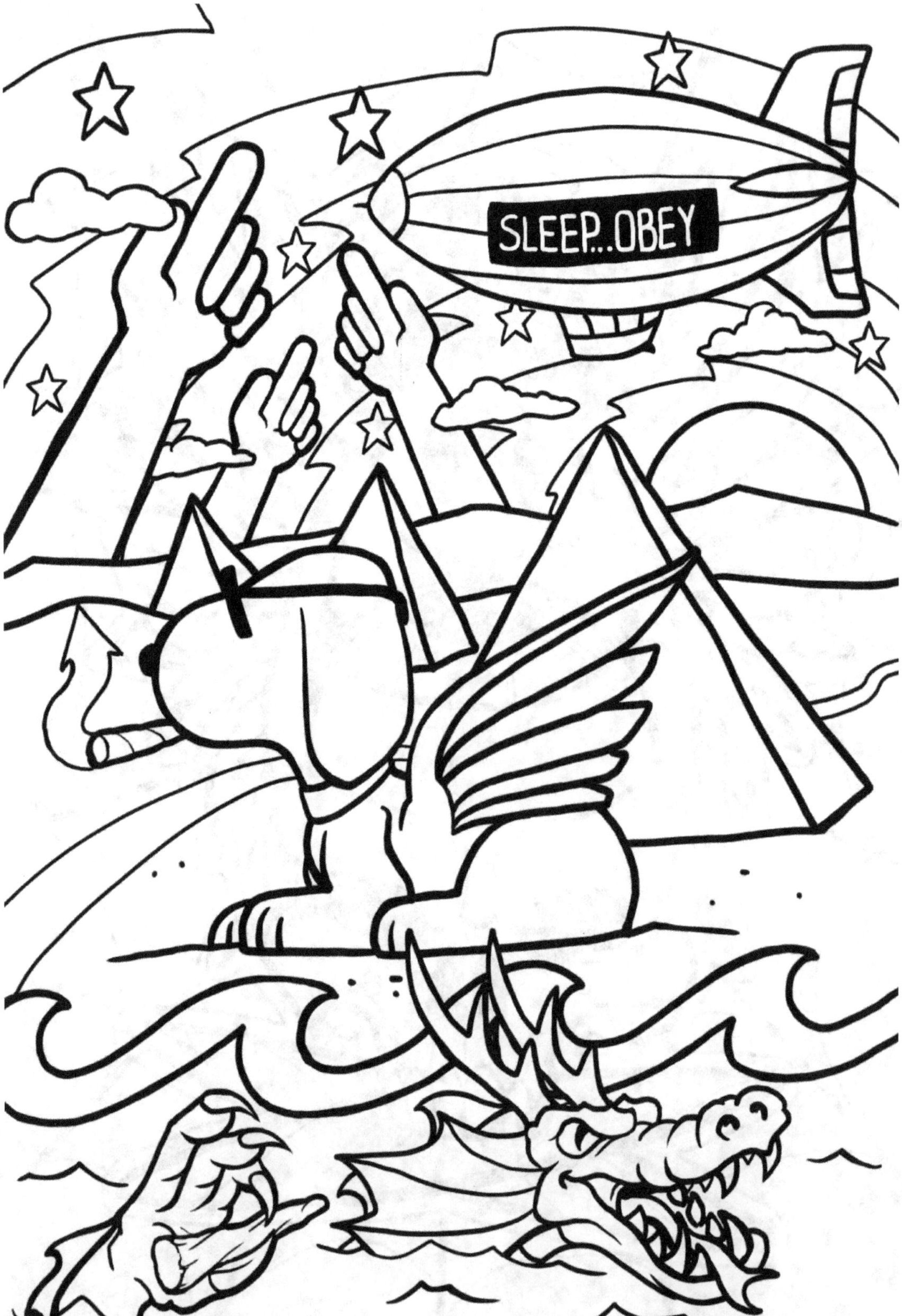
SLEEP...OBEY

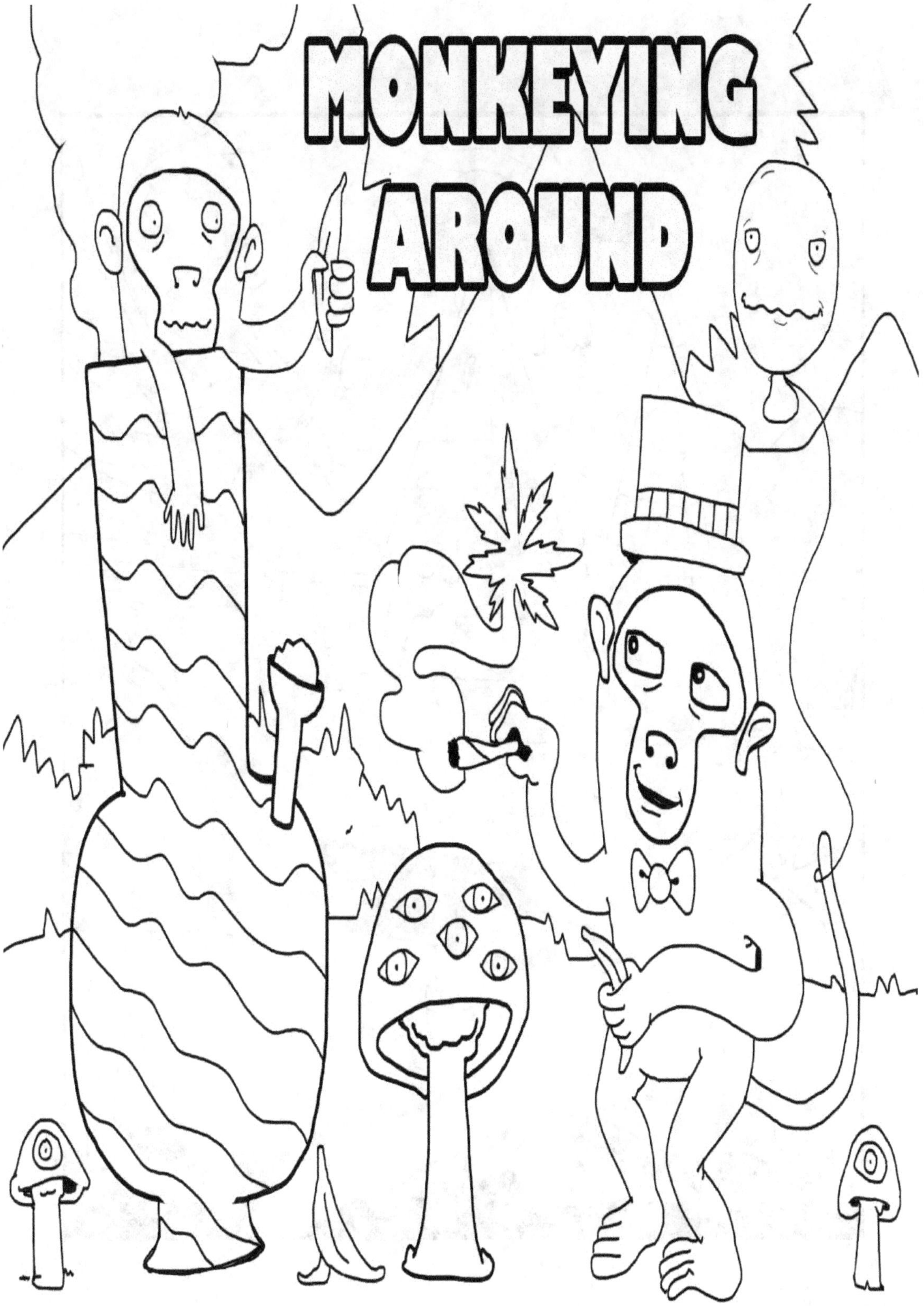
MONKEYING
AROUND

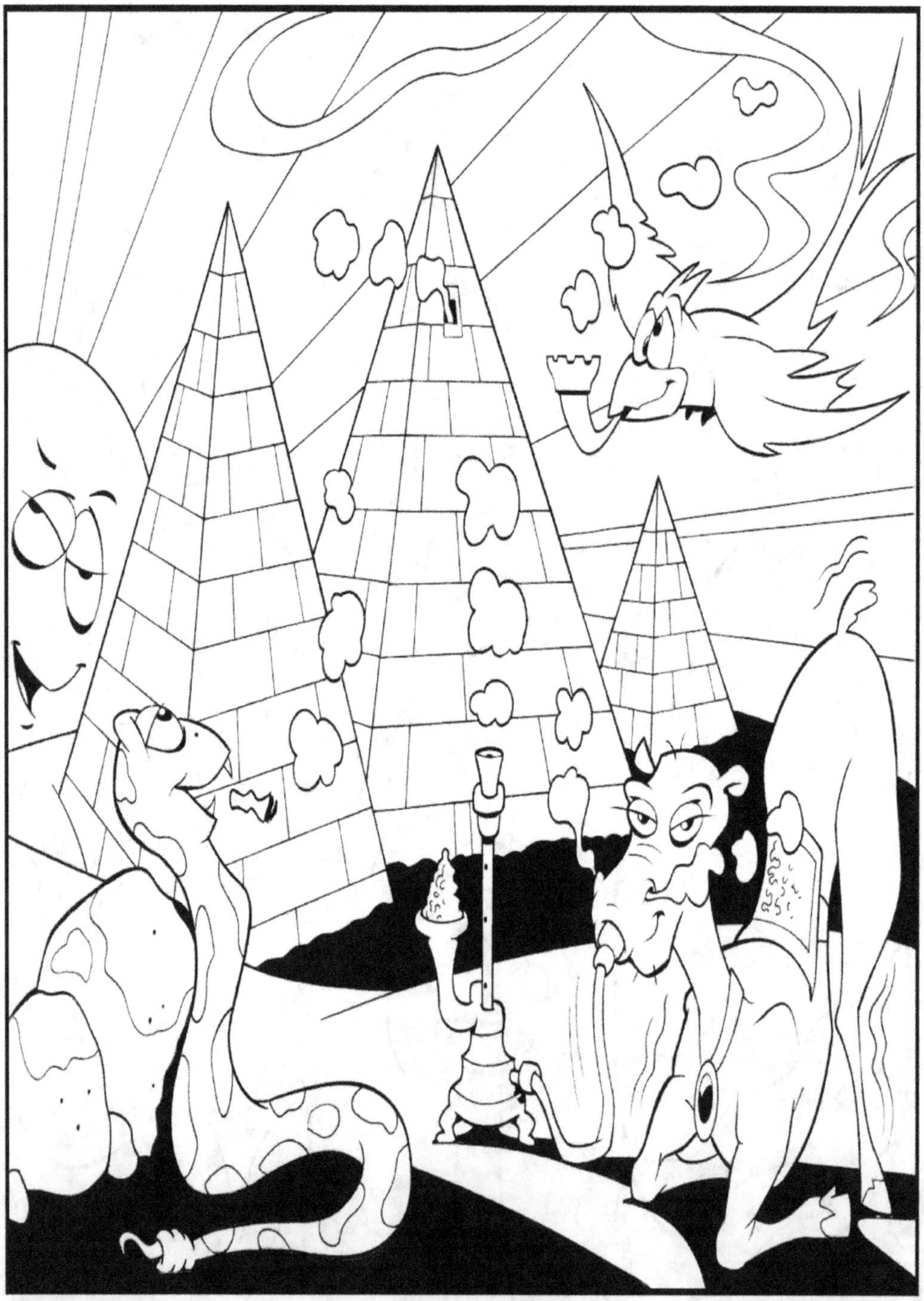

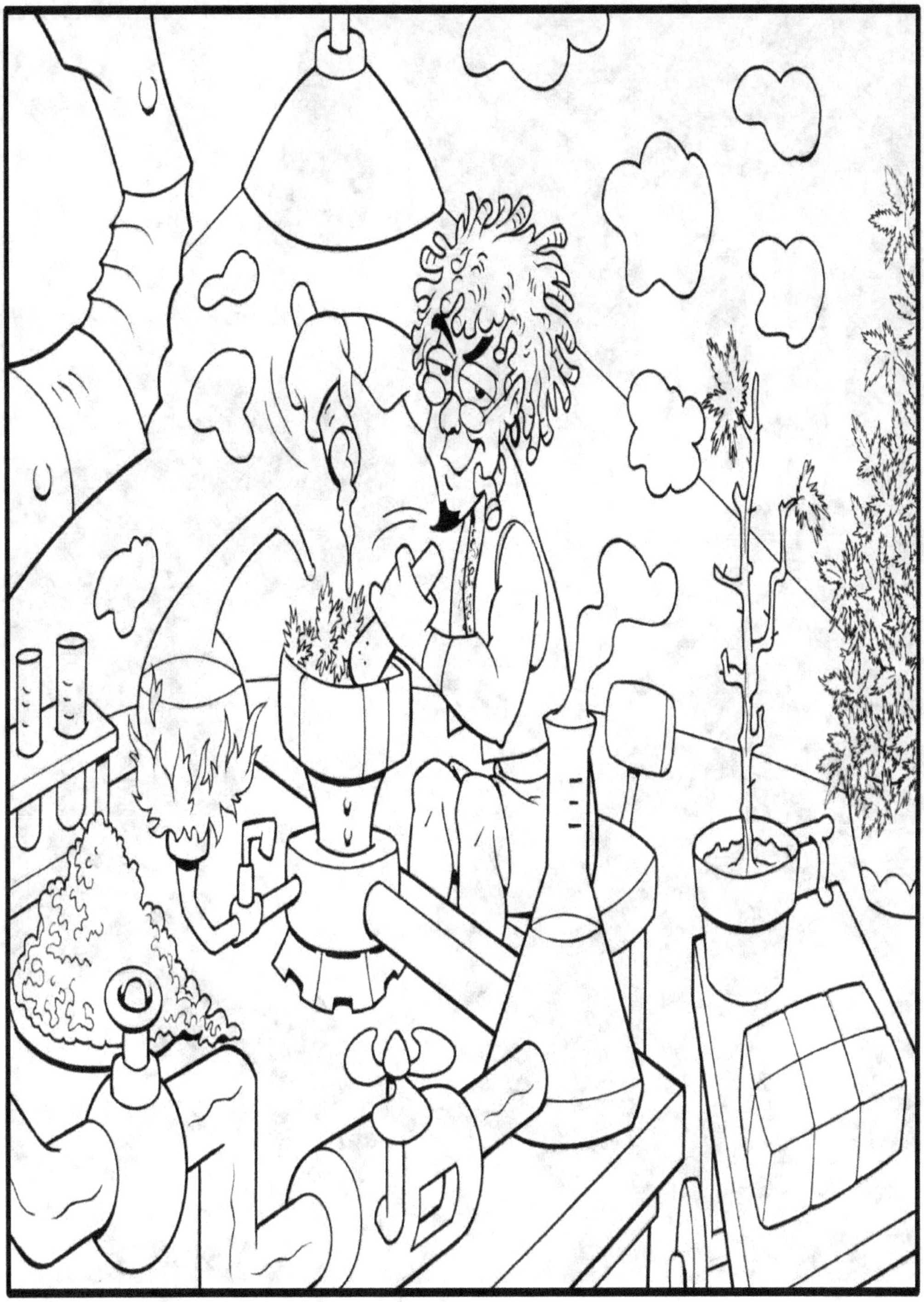

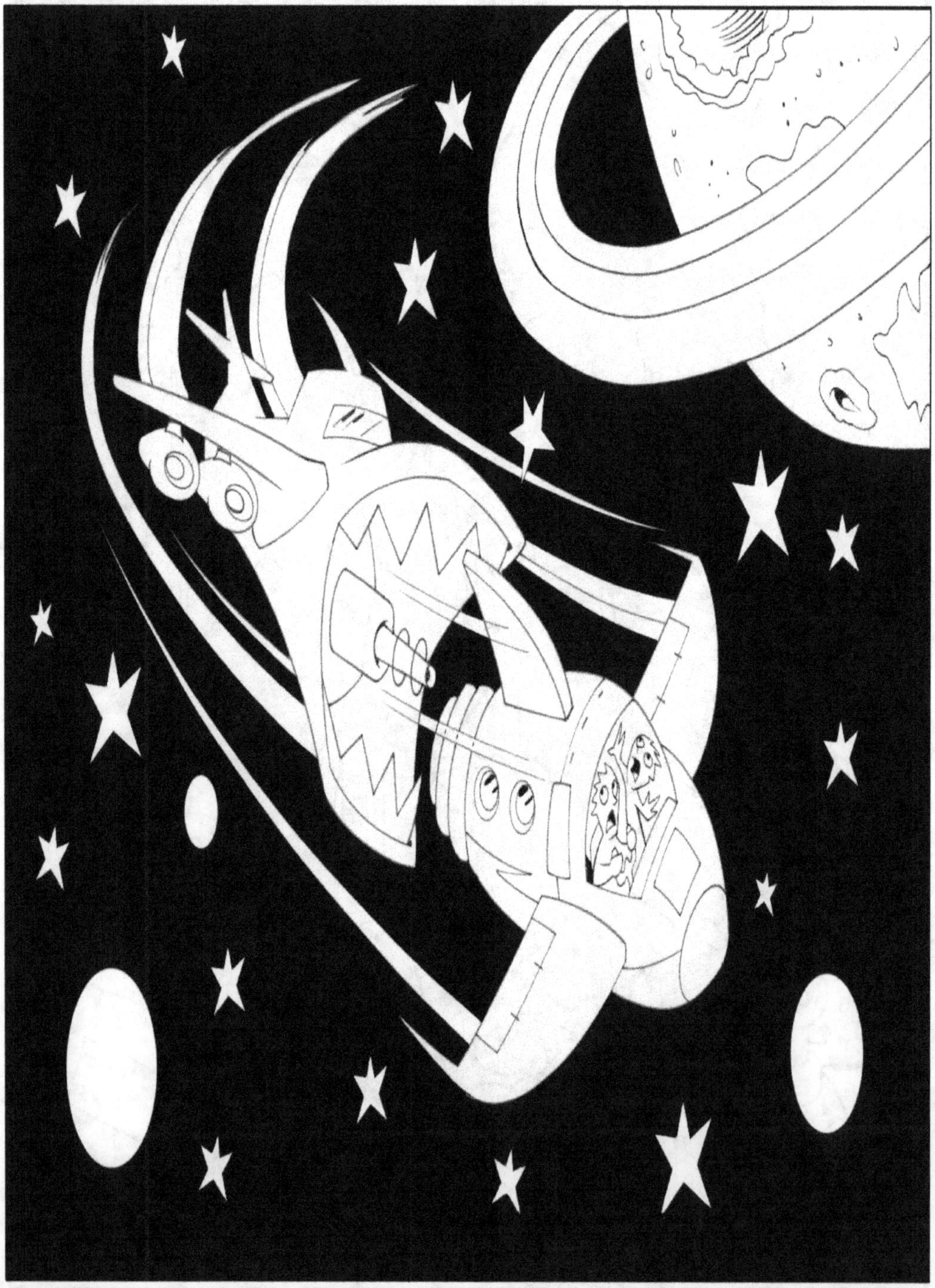

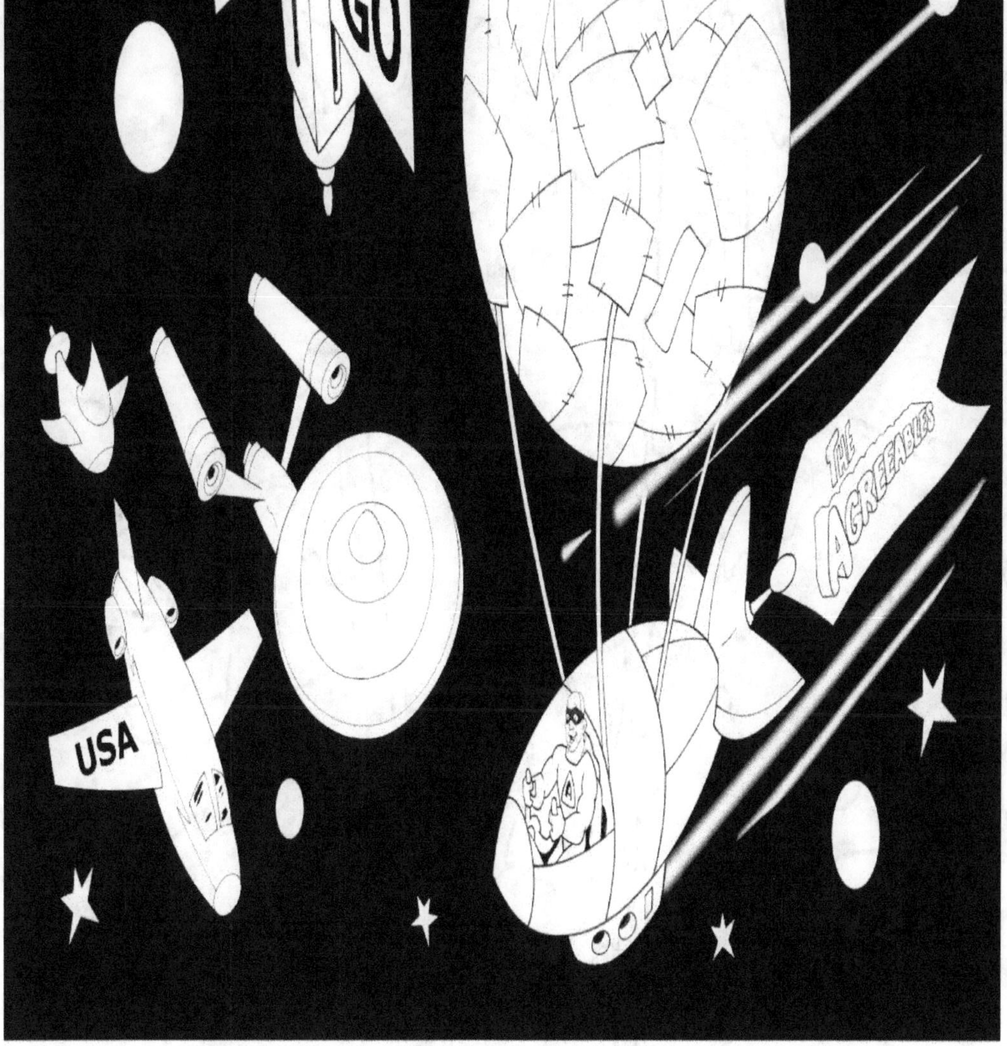
STOP
GO
USA
THE AGREEABLES

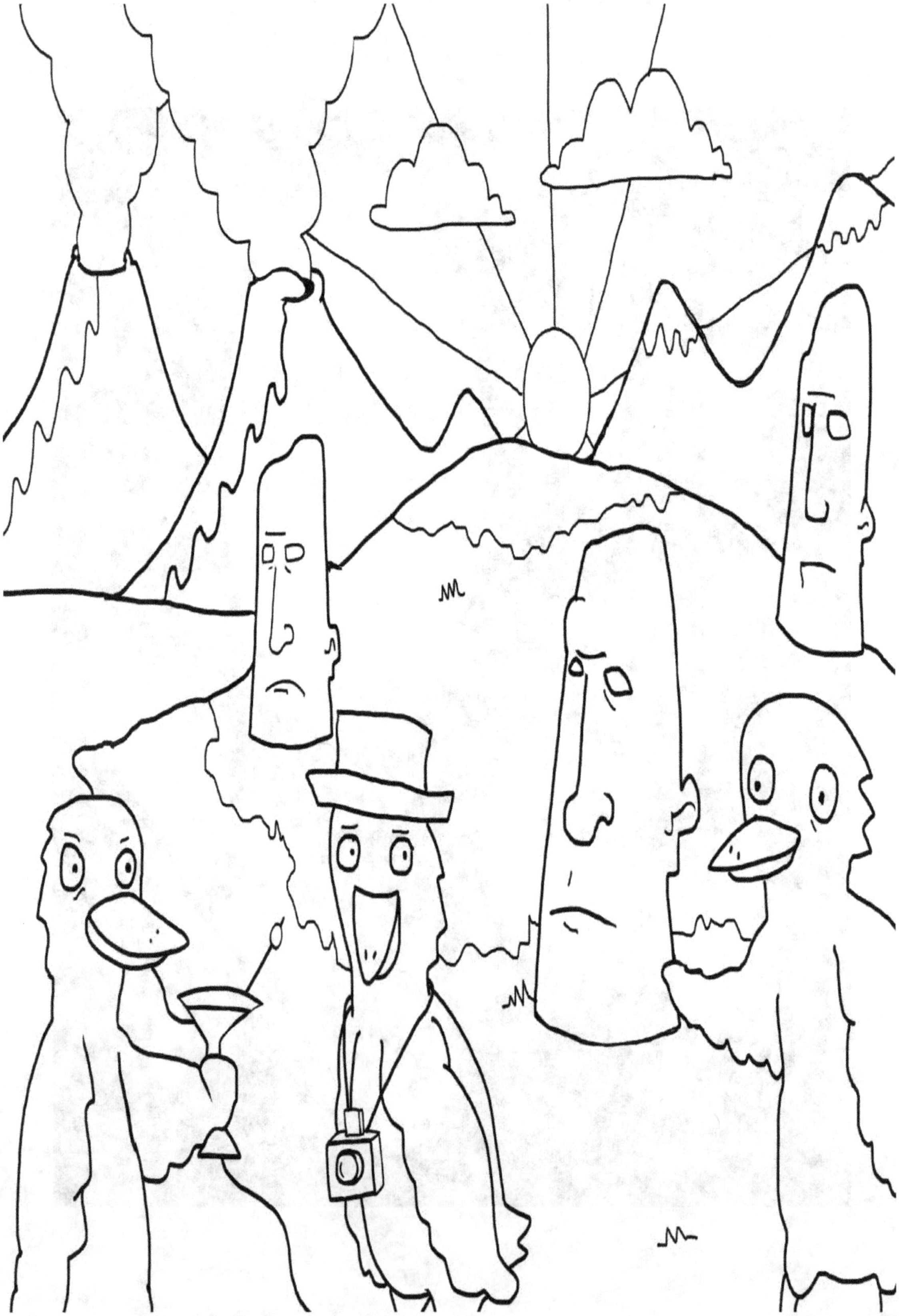

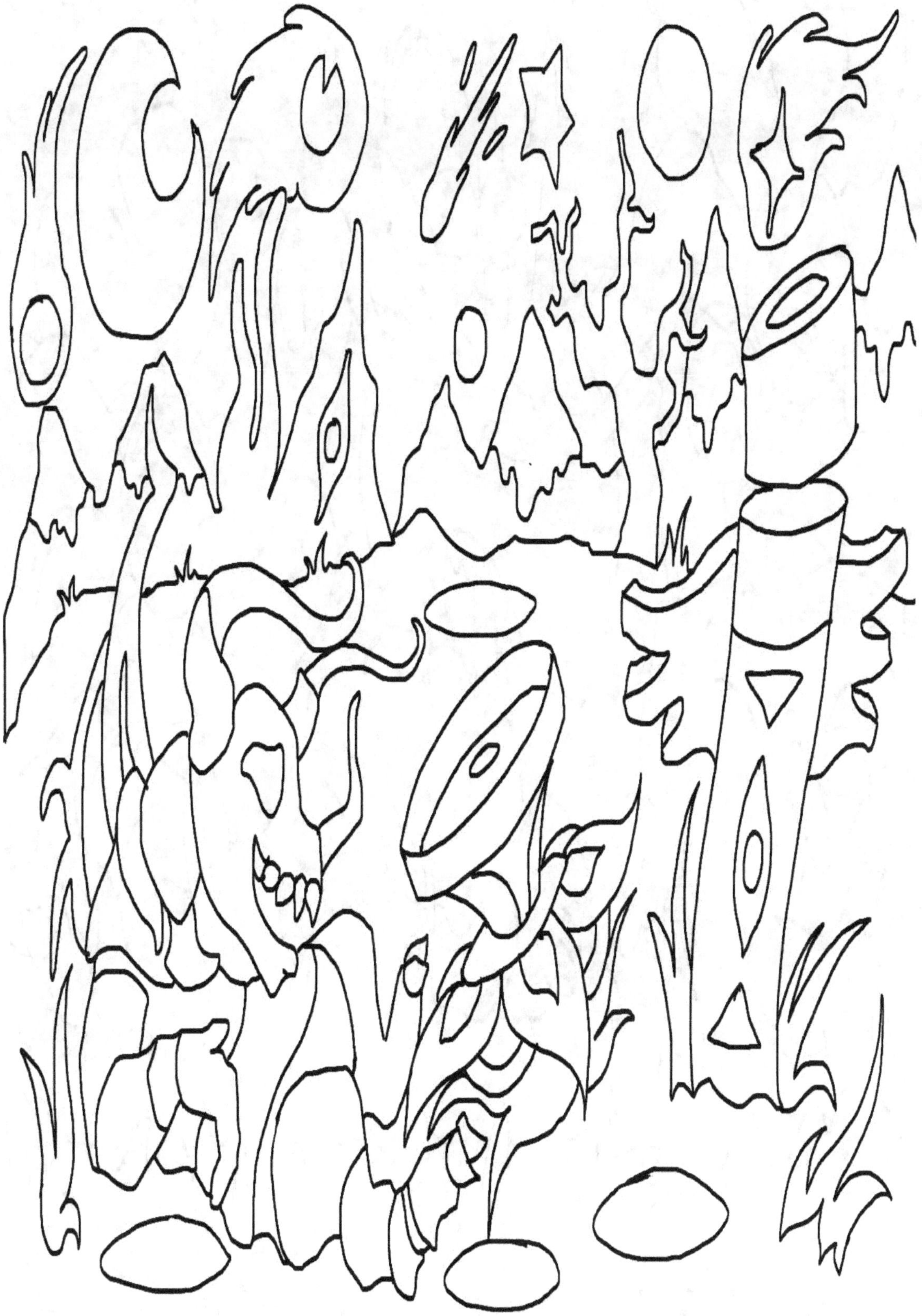

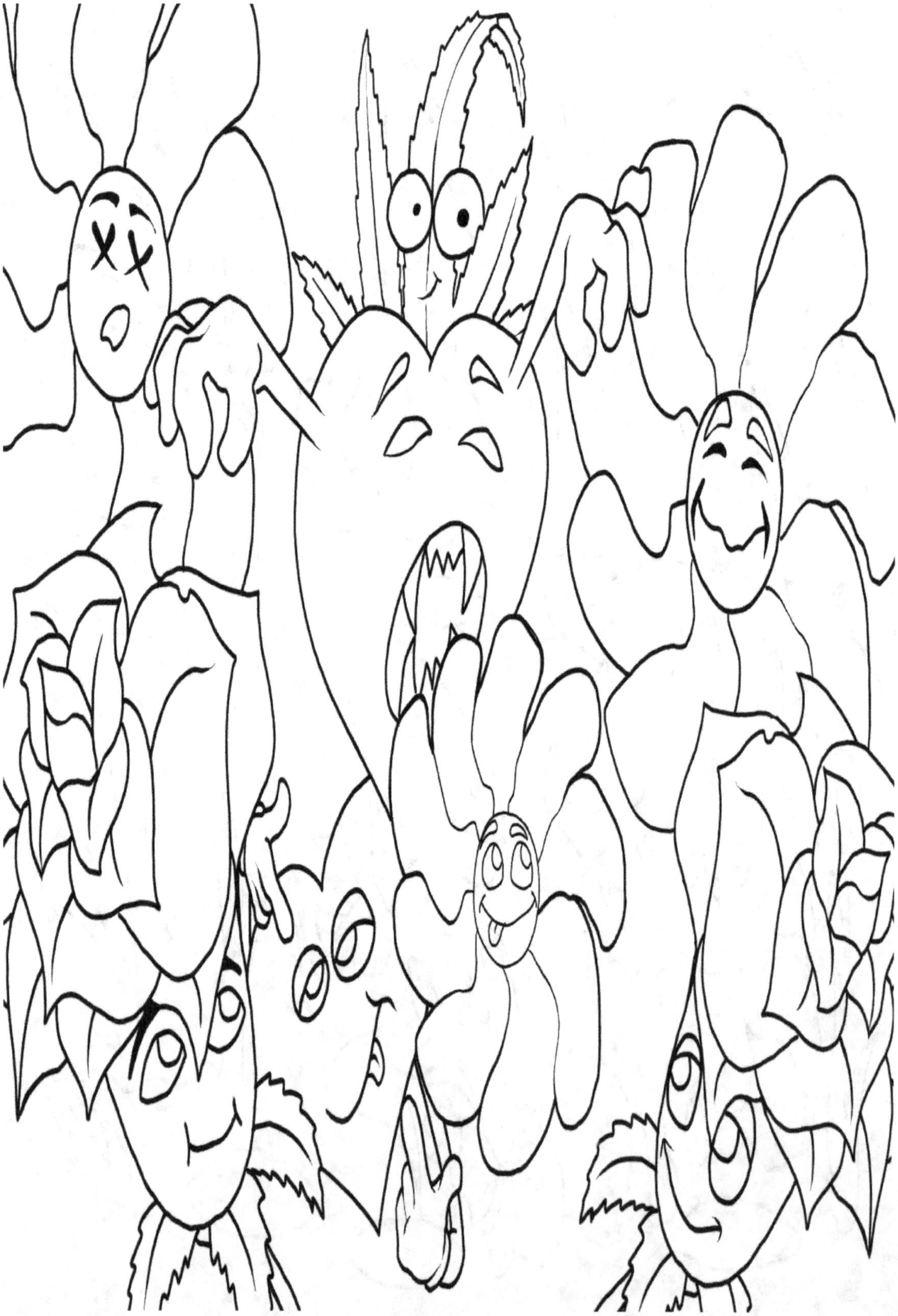

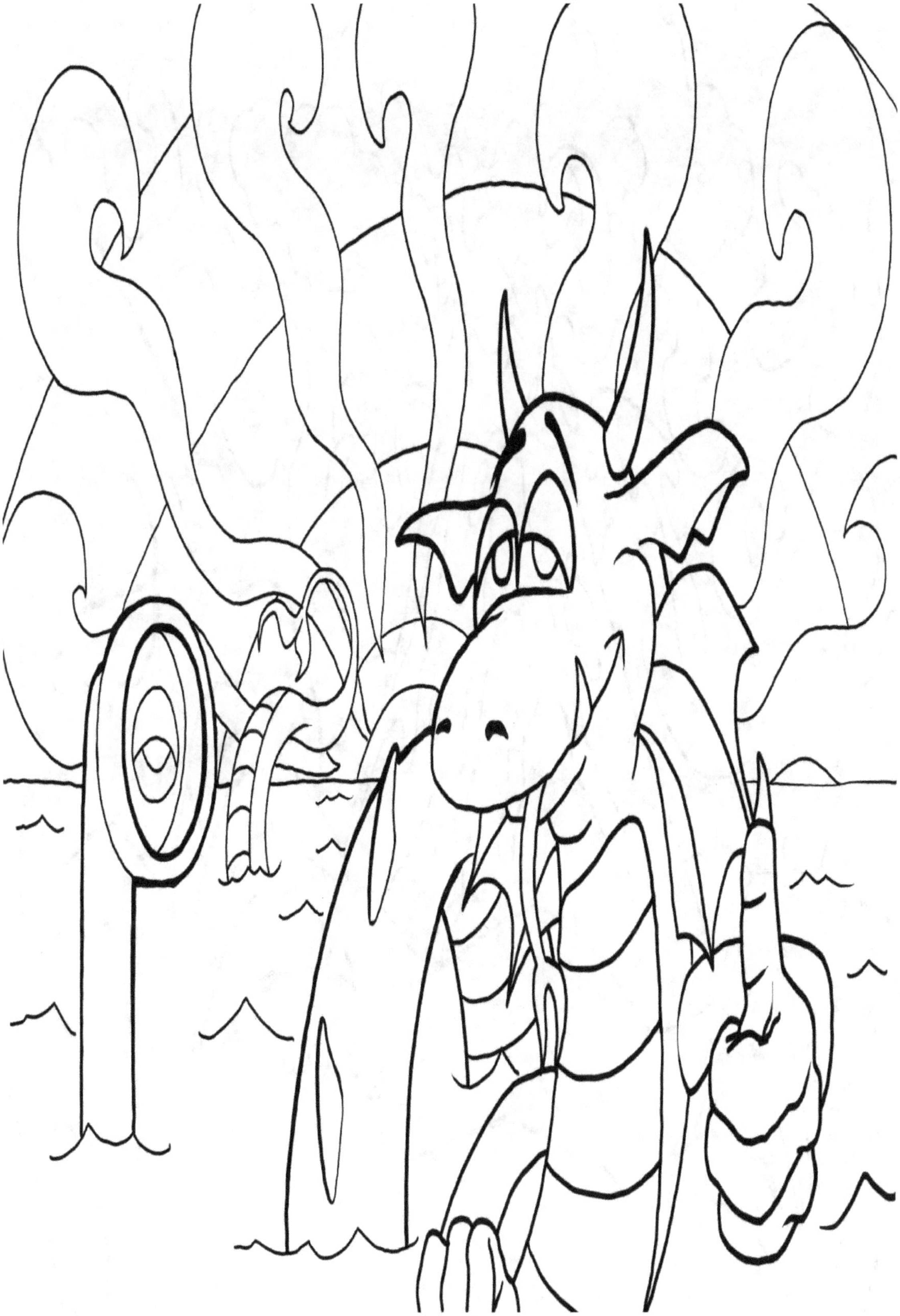

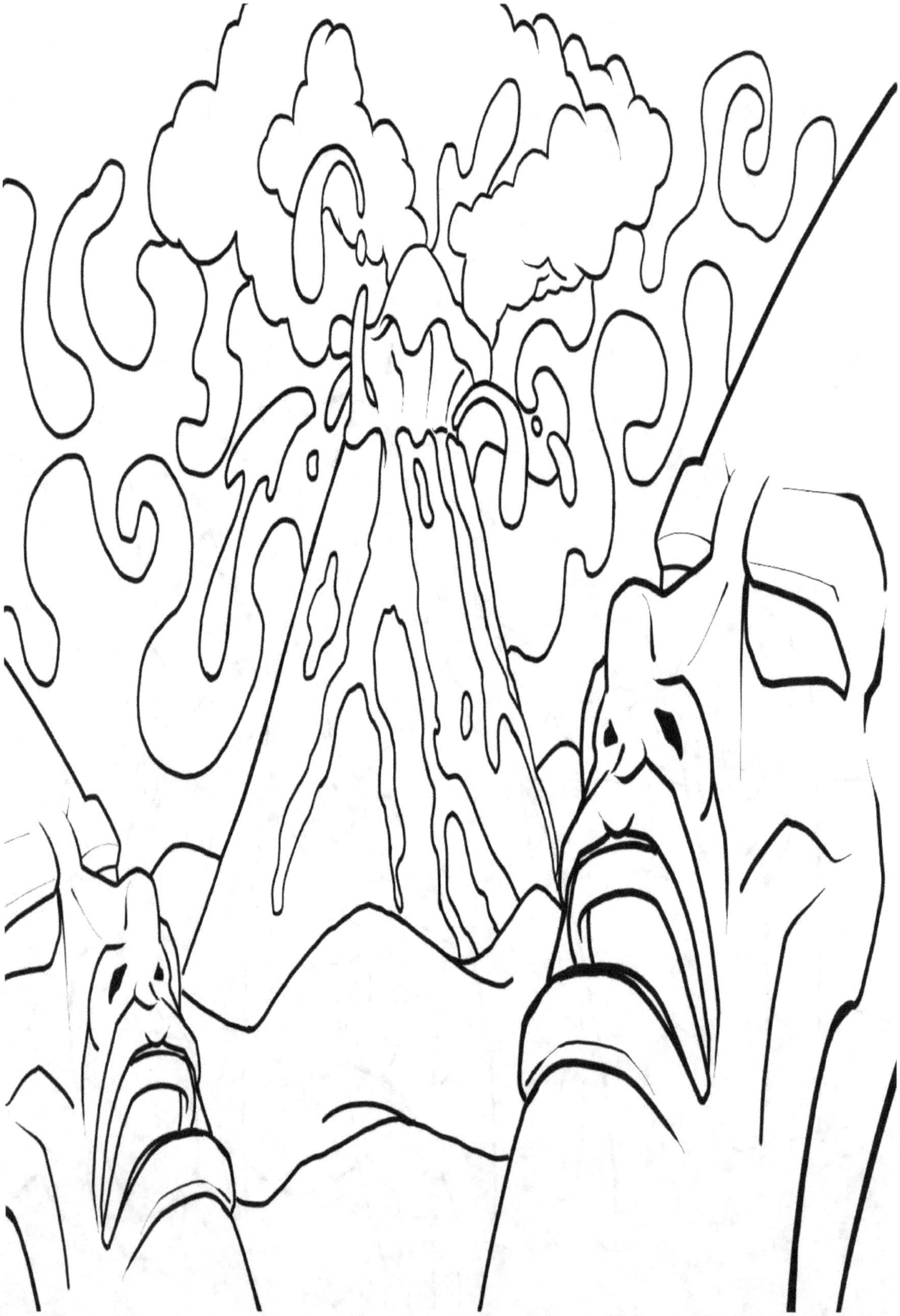

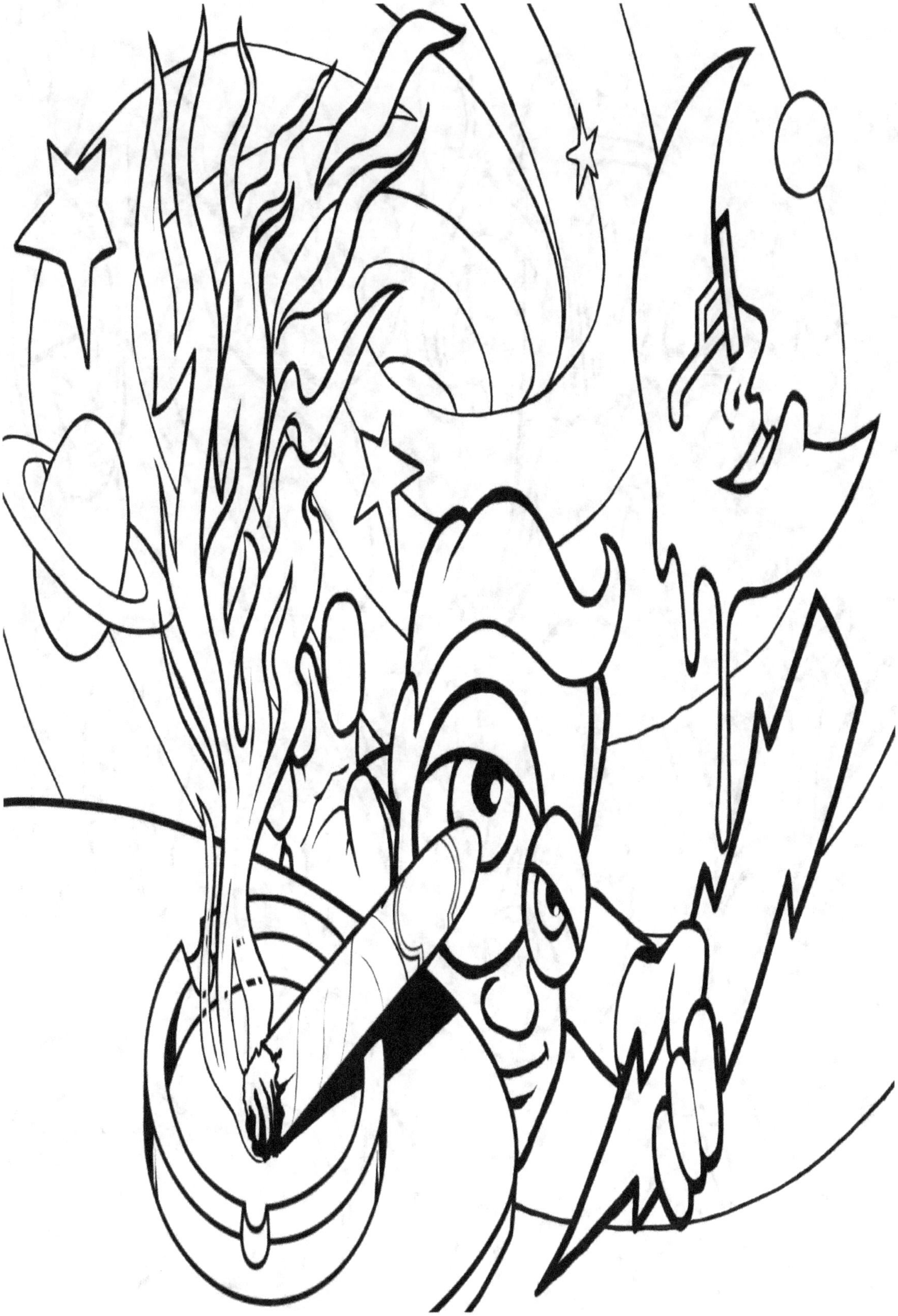

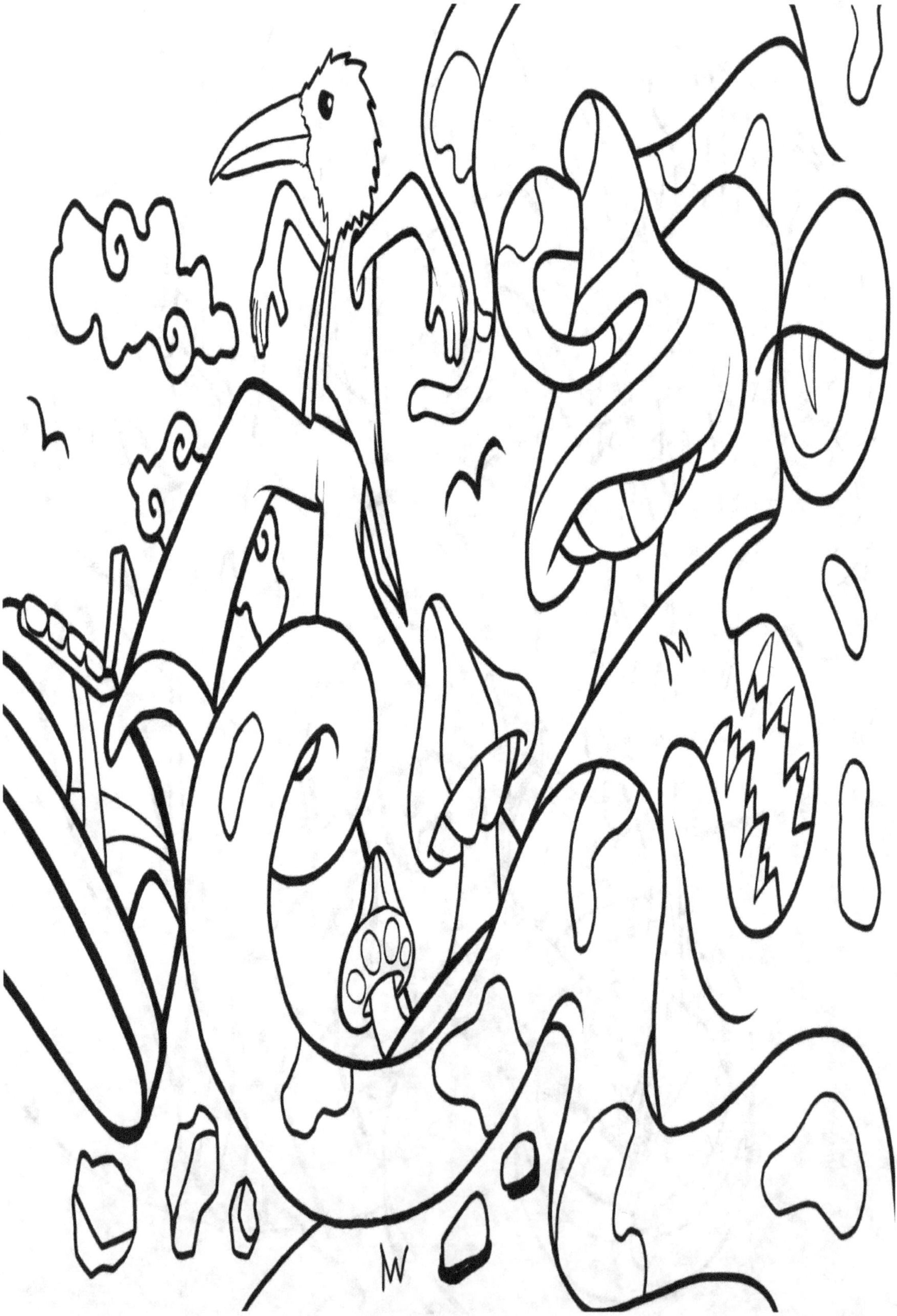

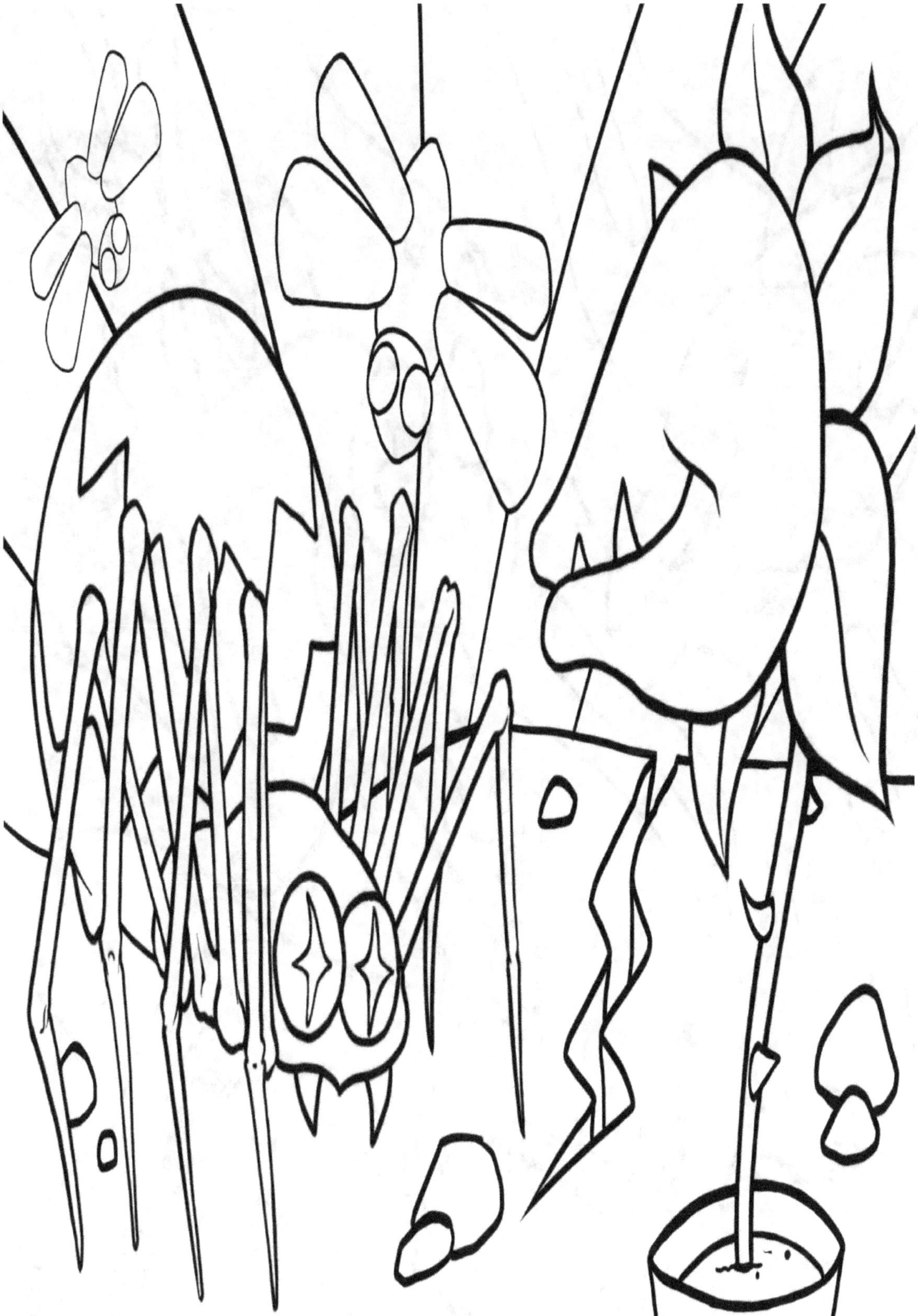

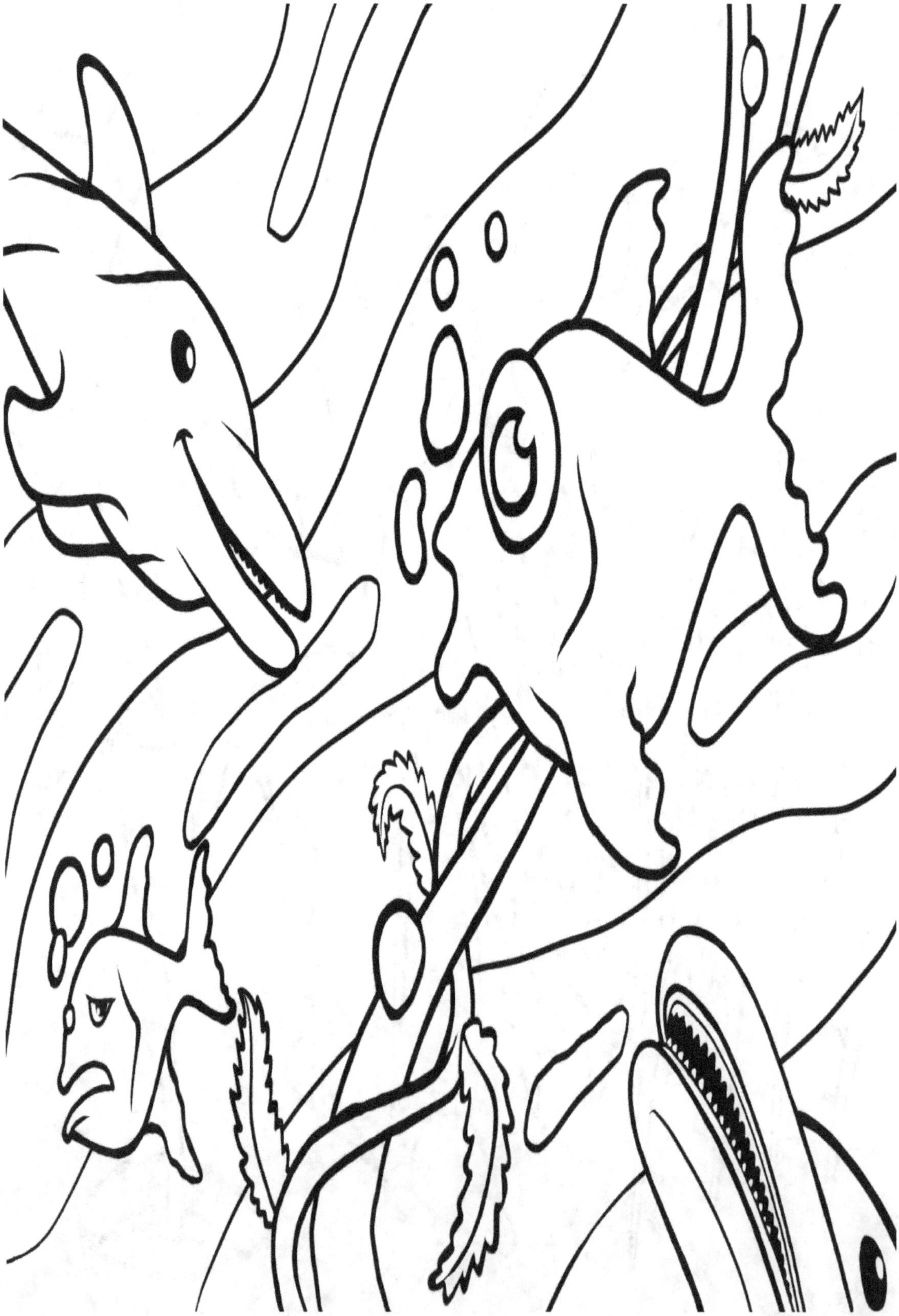

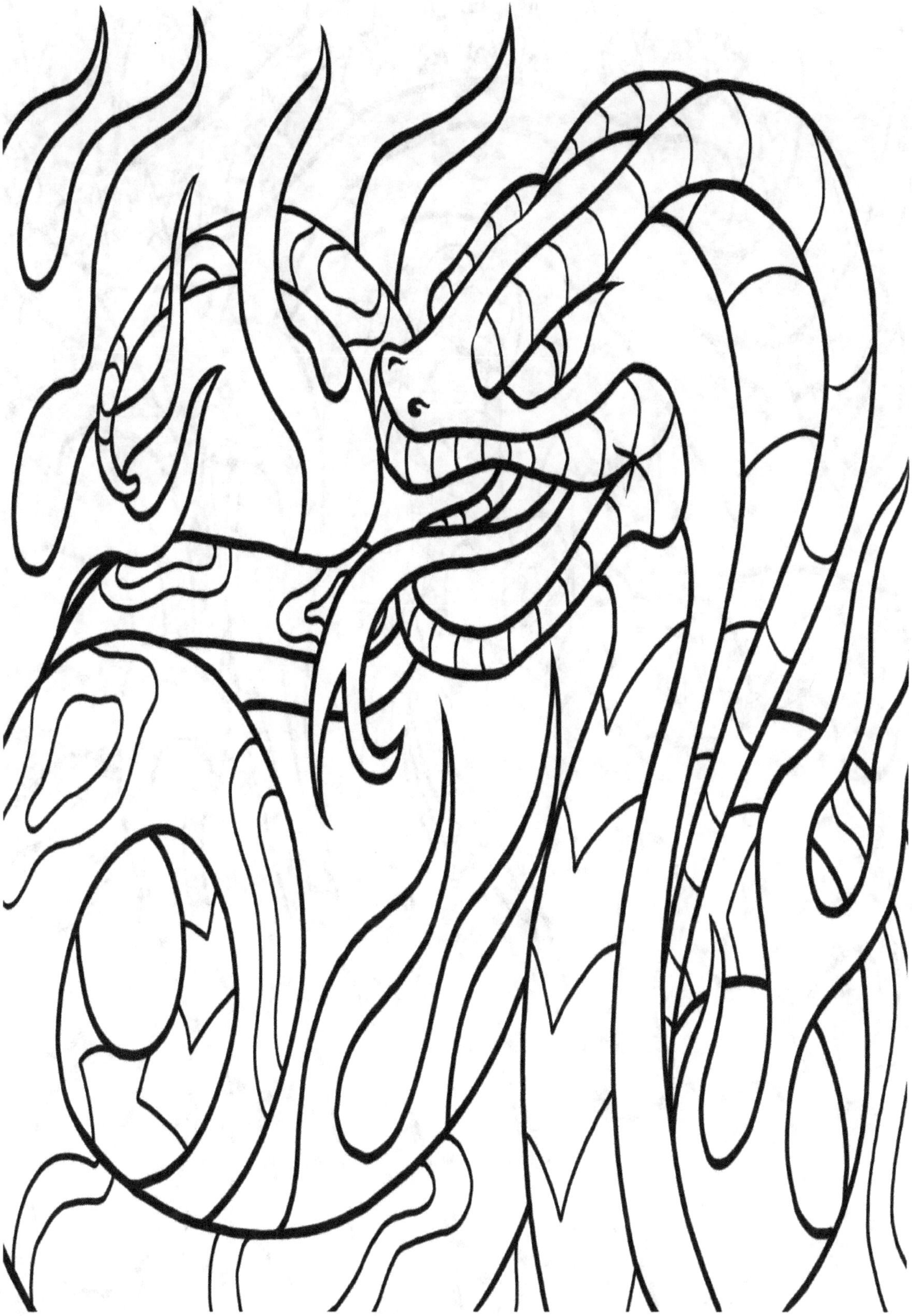

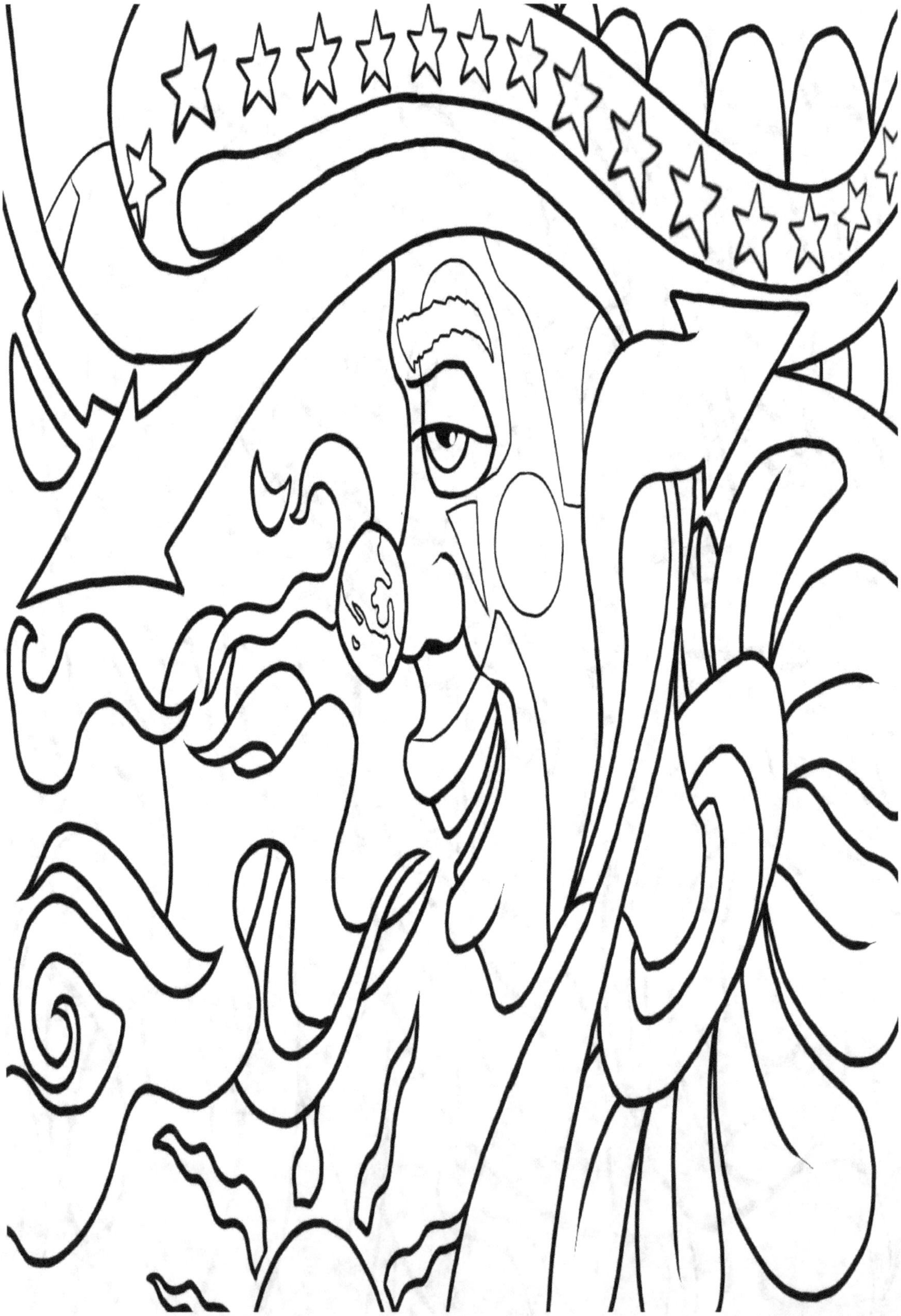

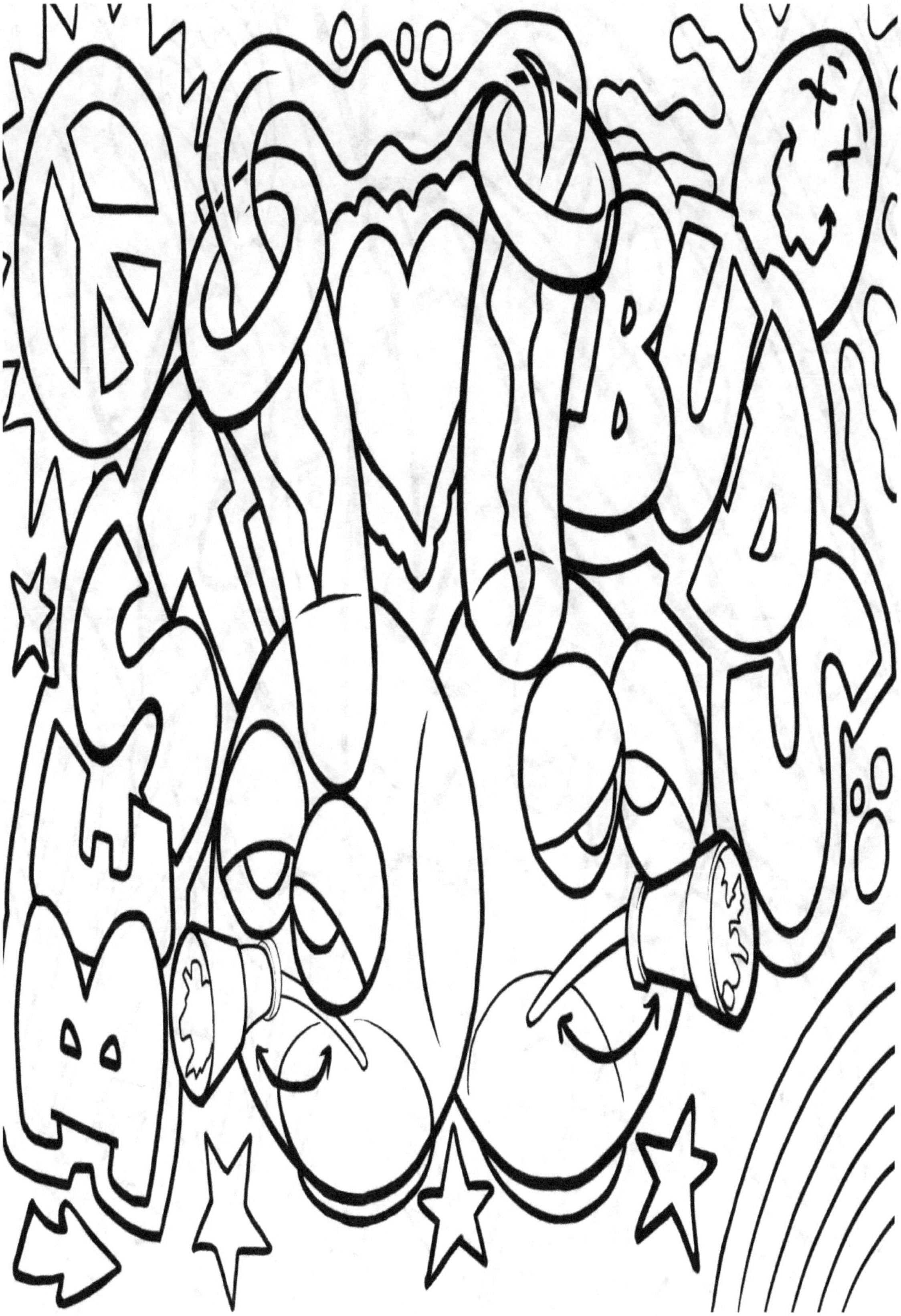

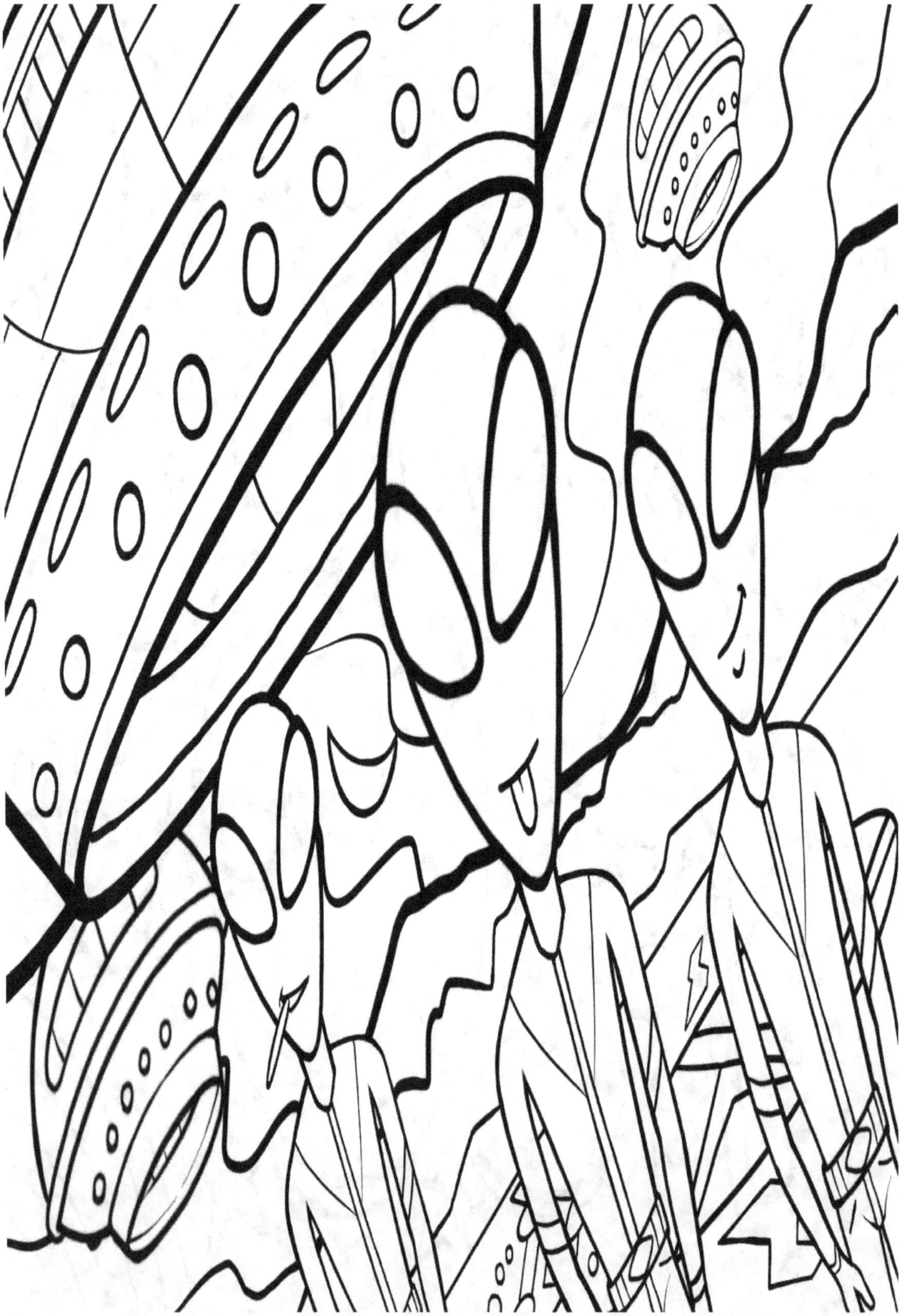

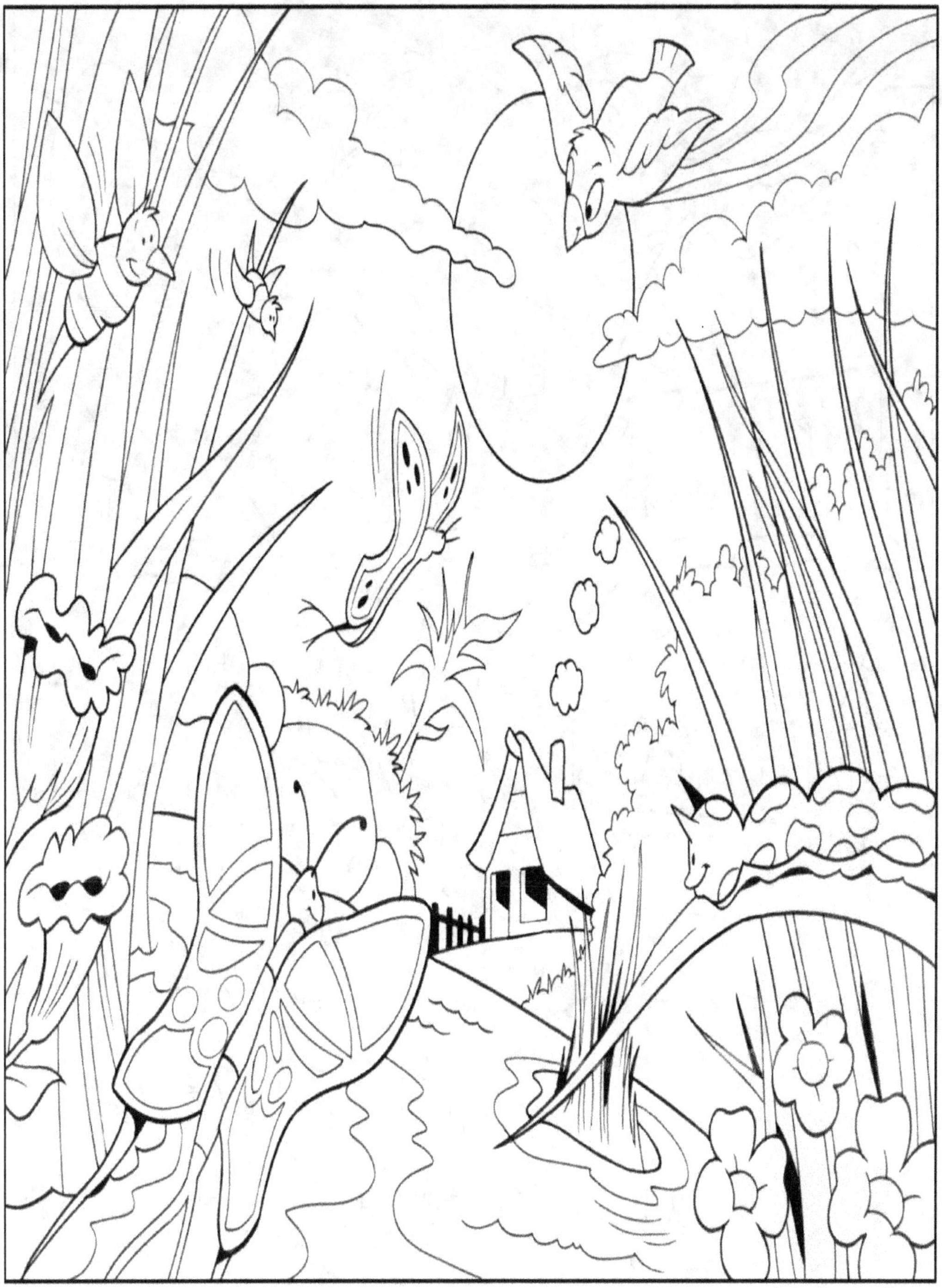

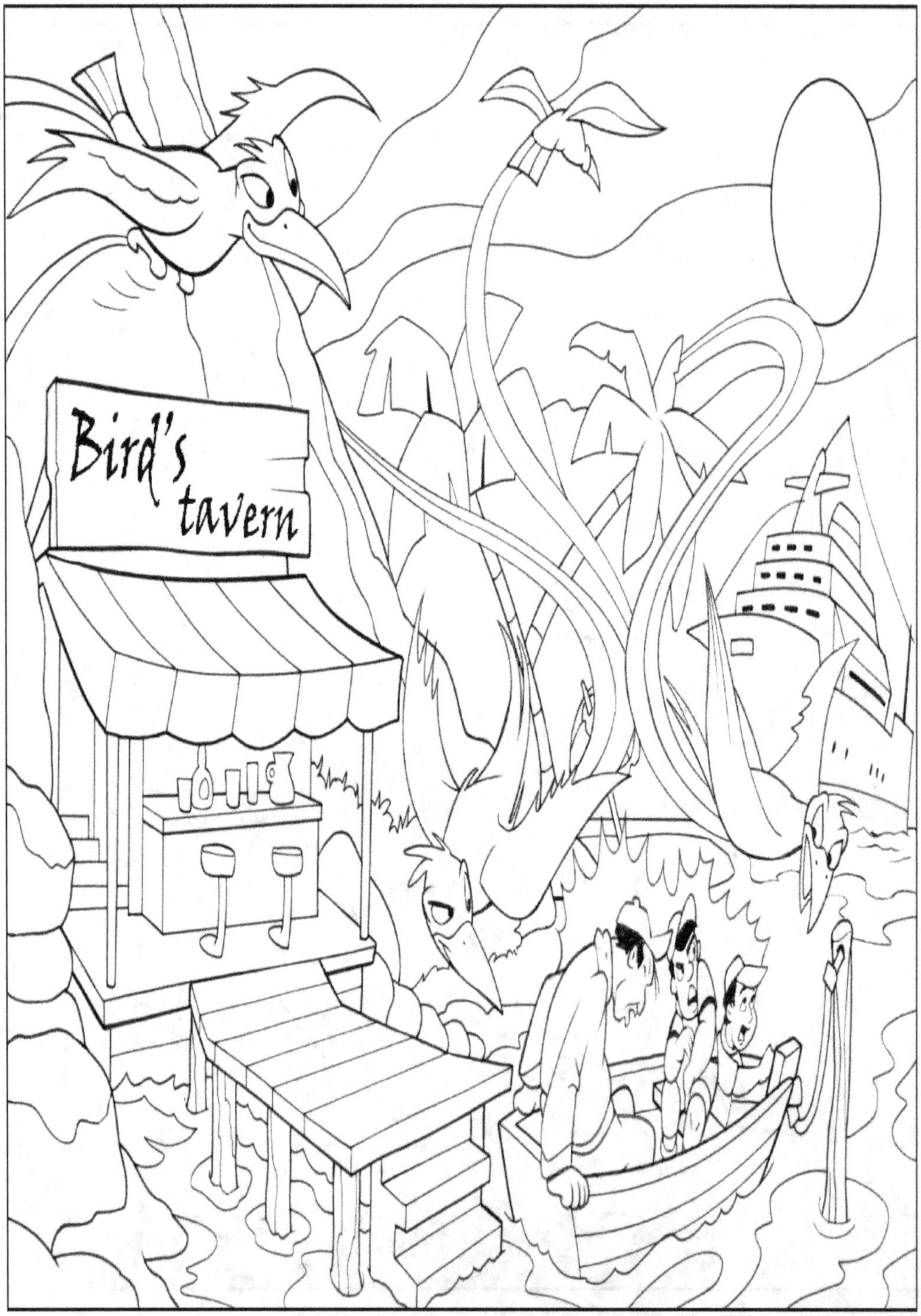
Bird's
tavern

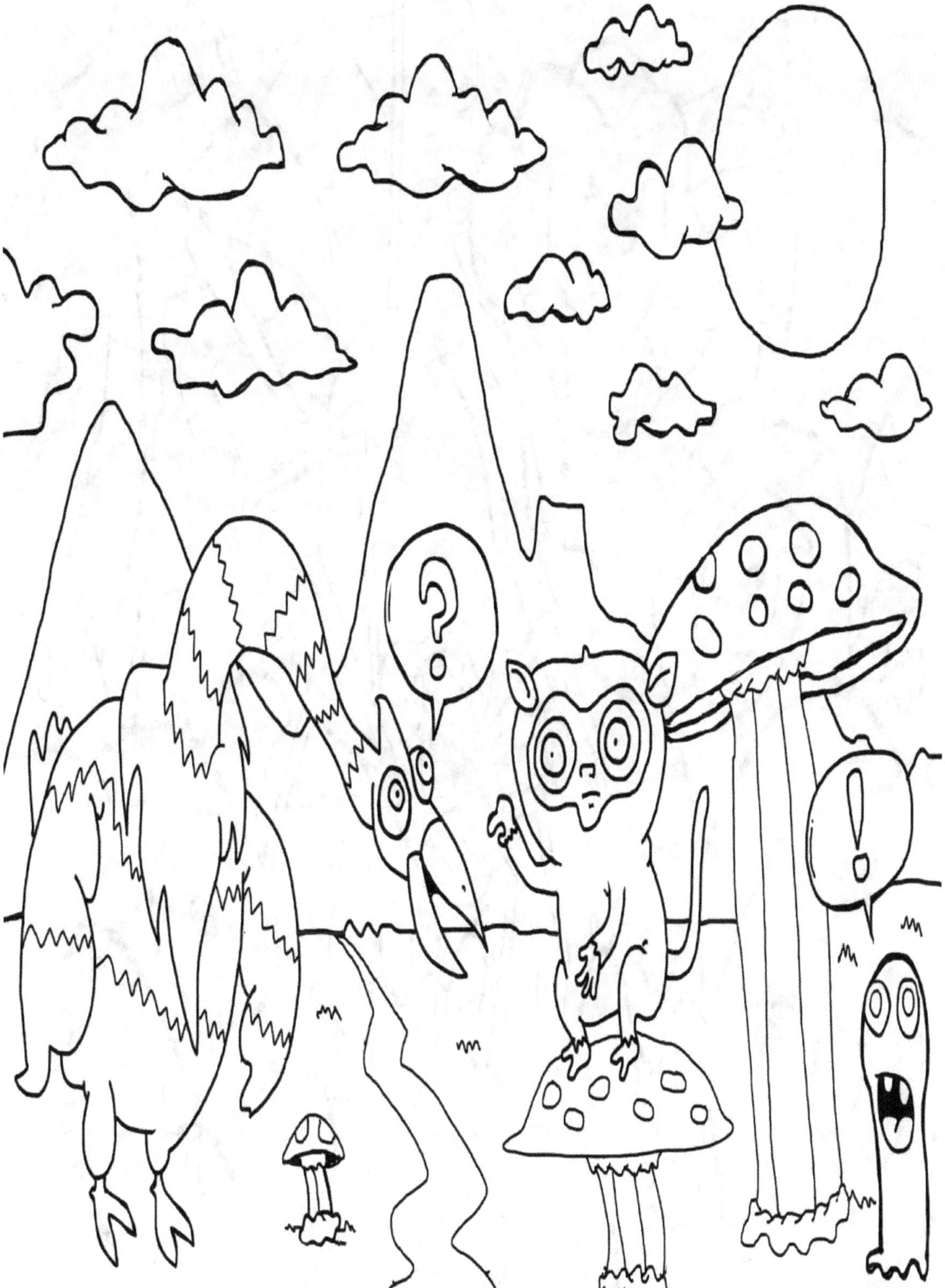

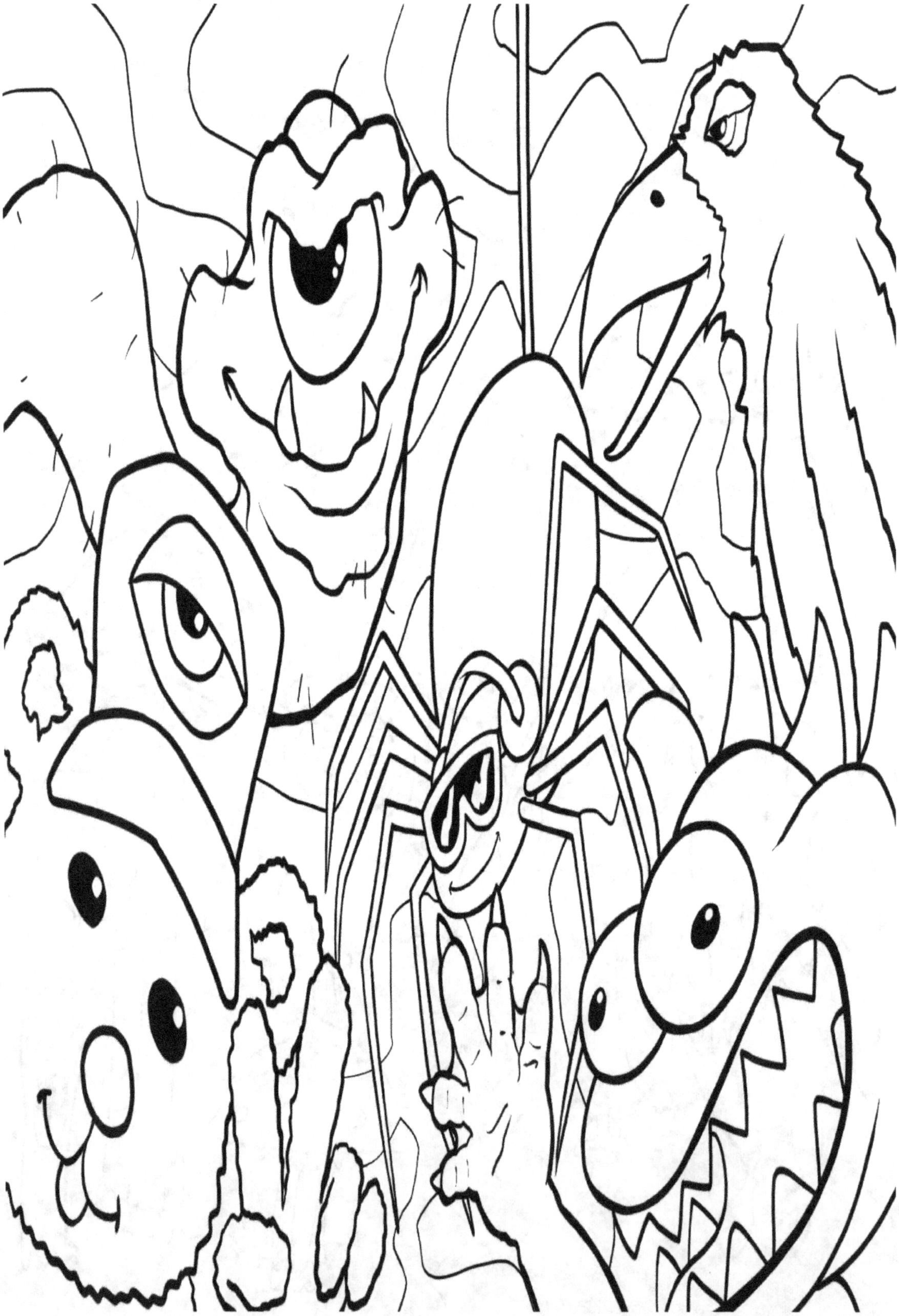

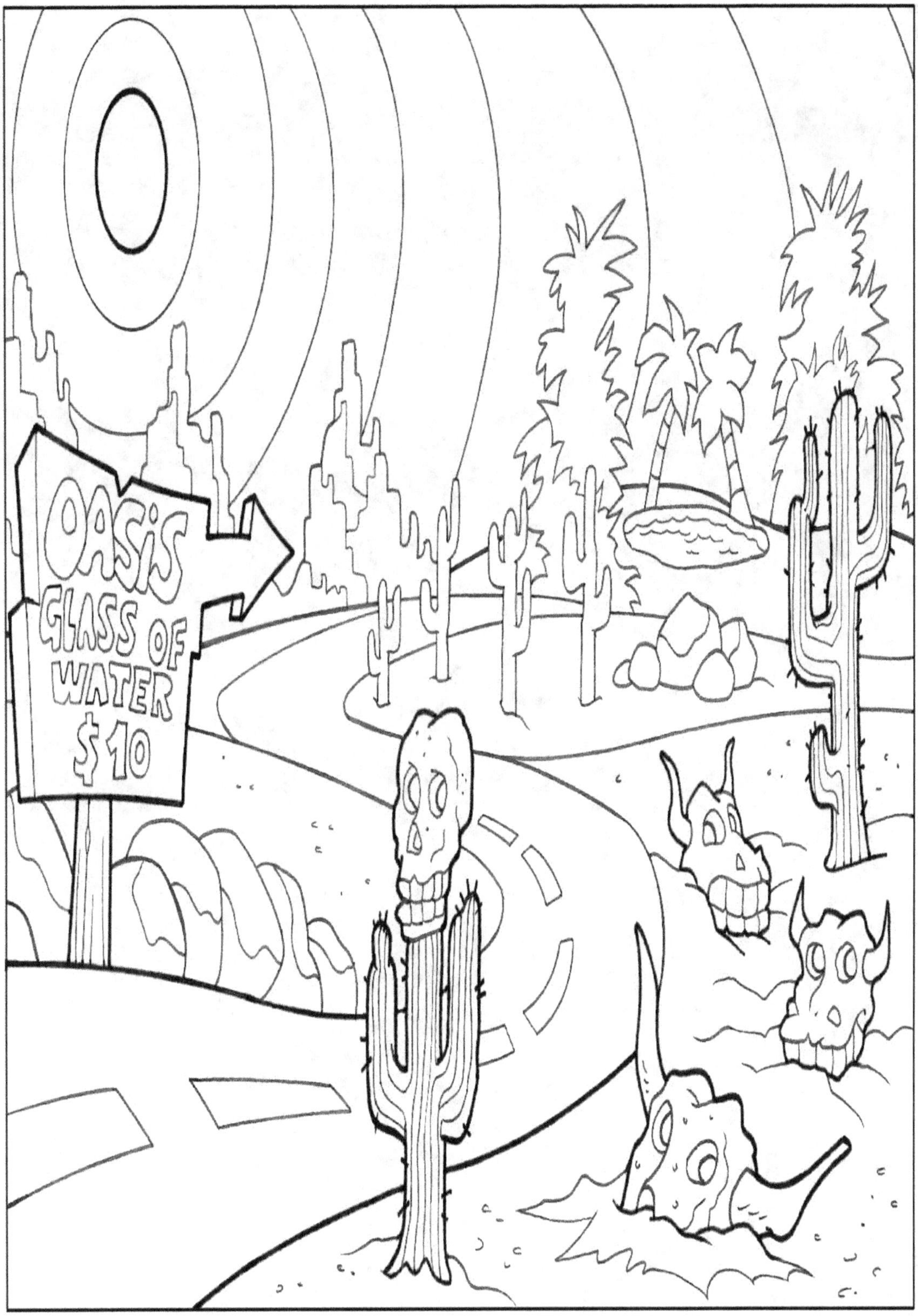
OASIS
GLASS OF WATER
$10

www.ingramcontent.com/pod-product-compliance
Lightning Source LLC
Chambersburg PA
CBHW081303180526
45170CB00007B/2552
* 9 7 8 1 5 2 3 3 7 0 3 2 0 *